Window-box Allotment

To my cousin Susan Cowdell who planted the first seed. And to the Encouragers: Shirley Hughes, Helen MacTaggart, Ann Schlee and The Monday Friends, my literary agent, Mike Shaw of Curtis Brown, and my Thrive Friends.
WITH LOVE

Window-box Allotment

A beginner's guide to container gardening

Penelope Bennett

Ebury Press
London

First published in 2001

1 3 5 7 9 10 8 6 4 2

Text copyright © Penelope Bennett 2001
Illustrations copyright © Pip Moon 2001

First published by Ebury Press
Random House, 20 Vauxhall Bridge Road, London SW1V 2SA

Random House Australia (Pty) Limited
20 Alfred Street, Milsons Point, Sydney, New South Wales 2061,
Australia

Random House New Zealand Limited
18 Poland Road, Glenfield, Auckland 10, New Zealand

Random House South Africa (Pty) Limited
Endulini, 5A Jubilee Road, Parktown 2193, South Africa

The Random House Group Limited Reg. No. 954009

www.randomhouse.co.uk

A CIP catalogue record for this book is available from the British Library

ISBN 0 09 187789 X

Editor: Mandy Greenfield
Designer: Ruth Prentice
Illustrator: Pip Moon
Indexer: Vicki Robinson

Printed and bound in Great Britain by Mackays of Chatham plc, Kent

"He who plants a garden plants happiness."

CHINESE PROVERB

Window boxes don't insist on being planted with petunias, geraniums and dusty rags of trailing ivy. They make equally good homes for vegetables and fruit. Growing now, in cold January, in window boxes, pots and hanging baskets on my west-facing, 16 x 9 ft (4.9 x 2.7 m) London roof-garden are Swiss chard, frizzy endive, pak choi, perpetual spinach, lamb's lettuce, garlic chives, rocket, mitsuba (a type of Japanese parsley), celeriac, winter purslane and curly-leaf parsley. There will be much more later in the year, such as dwarf beans, alpine strawberries, tomatoes, 'Salad Bowl' lettuce and aubergines. Most of the vegetables growing now were sown last spring and autumn, except for the spinach and Swiss chard, which were sown two years ago.

Almost everyone can have a miniature allotment. Young, small hands and elderly, stiff hands can 'dig' (or trowel-dig) compost that is only a few inches deep. For those who cannot see, window boxes and pots are easy for fingers to 'walk' over and examine. They're also good for backs that can't and backs that can bend; for those who find sitting (especially in a wheelchair) easier; and for those who prefer kneeling or standing. And for people who live in window ledge-less flats, there is seed-sprouting to try (see pages 186-194). Only a small investment is needed – hardly an overdraft – and this can be made month by month.

Both people without and people with gardens can enjoy window-box gardening because it is quite different from 'garden gardening'. Unless you're a snail or a worm, you can't *see* seeds sprouting: the eyes are too far away from the ground. But containers can be placed at eye-level and are on a small scale. Because such gardening is intimate, you are more a part of it and can observe more of what is going on, particularly through a magnifying glass: the cucumber slowly fattening and lengthening, the alpine strawberry flower mysteriously changing into fruit. Although it is small, the enjoyment, interest and enrichment it produces are great.

I am not a horticulturist, just an enthusiastic beginner. What follow are not intended to be dictatorial directions, but simply suggestions, which may be followed, partly followed or ignored.

What is growing now

January is too cold and dark to sow seeds, except parsley for a trial seed-sowing and – says the seed packet – 'Gardeners' Delight' tomatoes, though it seems a little early, but this depends on where you live and what the weather is like. January is a good time, however, to start preparing for all the seed sowing and planting you will be doing in the coming warmer months.

Now is the time for preparation

Start collecting small mustard-and-cress-sized plastic super-market containers (measuring about 6 x 4 x 2 inches or 15 x 10 x 5 cm), preferably transparent ones, because lengthening roots are interesting to watch. Larger containers – those in which those concrete-like supermarket peaches are sold, for instance – can also be useful for more vigorous seeds and beans. Also collect the cardboard cores of toilet rolls. These make good runner bean germination cylinders.

Buy some seed-sowing or multi-purpose compost. As you will not only be admiring the results of your sowing but eating them too, buy organic compost unless you find appealing the idea of garnishing your food with sprinklings of artificial fertilisers. Only a little is needed, but begin with the best.

organic

The *Oxford English Dictionary* definition: a fertiliser or manure produced from natural substances usually without the addition of chemicals; an equivalent of the word 'living'. Julian Huxley (1887–1975) English biologist and humanist.

One knows these words as acquaintances the definitions just deepen the acquaintanceship.

Get a small sieve, approximately 6 inches (15 cm) in diameter, for sifting soil. Buy some wipe-clean plant labels and an indelible pen. Invest in the smallest electric propagator. Alternatively, if you're uncertain whether you're going to enjoy window-box gardening, buy a full-sized seed tray with a transparent plastic lid, or a roll of clingfilm. To prevent the spread of disease, everything should first be washed in a mild solution of household bleach or sterilising solution, then thoroughly rinsed. This is pleasurable winter-hibernation work on a cold, dark day – hands in warm, soapy water. It makes January a more friendly month and brings spring forward. All that is needed now is time to study the seed catalogues.

Fear of sowing

It is astonishing how many grown-up people have never sown a single seed. The idea of seed-sowing seems to fill them with trepidation, as though it is some magical process (which, of course, it is in a way) only for the cognoscenti, and from which they are excluded. In fact seed sowing is one of the simplest things to do. If birds and breezes can do it, it should not be beyond humans, and besides 75 per cent of the work is done by the seeds themselves.

Trial parsley-seed sowing

For those who have never done any sowing, January is a good time to practise, before the real seed-sowing months arrive. Despite the saying that parsley should be sown naked (the sower, not the parsley) by moonlight – when it's warm outside – it can also be sown successfully indoors, when you are fully clothed and during daylight. It is one of the few plants that can be germinated indoors all year round.

It is not necessary to have a potting shed, greenhouse or anywhere special to sow seeds. All that's needed is a table spread with newspaper.

The following basic instructions apply to sowing most of the seeds mentioned in this book.

1 Make drainage holes in the bottom of one of the plastic supermarket containers (some are already pierced), piercing them from the inside out to make certain the drainage works.

2 Crumble away any lumps in the compost, then sieve it into the container until it overflows. The compost needs to be fine and friable (easily crumbled) to create a comfortable bed for the seeds and their roots to grow in – imagine yourself living in it. For those who are fond of their hands and don't like the idea of touching compost, rub them with barrier cream before resorting to gloves, this at least lets the hands feel what they are touching, whereas gloves do not, a large proportion of the pleasure being on the other side of the glove – one might as well wear gloves while making love.

3 Level the surface of the compost with something straight, such as a ruler.

4 Gently firm the compost down with your palm. Seeds need something firmish, but not rock-hard, to rest on.

5 Put the filled container into the sink (or a bigger receptacle), then fill the sink with water until it comes halfway up the container's sides. Leave until the

compost has drunk its fill and glistens on top, like coal. Remove and allow to drain. Watering before sowing avoids disturbing the seeds and makes their sowing simpler, as they are more visible against the water-darkened compost. It also makes it easier to see how much soil to sieve on top. A 6 x 4 x 2 inch (15 x 10 x 5 cm) container will take only about fifteen seeds, or fewer. (Another advantage of pot and box gardening is that a single packet of seeds can last for several years. Parsley seeds given to me five years ago are still germinating and seeds of an Arctic lupin have been known to grow after lying in the ground for 10,000 years.)

6 Some seeds, such as Virginia stock (a few flowers have been included for the sake of their scent or colour), prefer to be sown on the surface of the compost and left uncovered. Others need more privacy and require a covering of soil. The seed packet instructions usually indicate the seeds' needs.

7 Italian plain-leaved parsley seeds are greyish and rowing boat-shaped. Mark out five evenly spaced rows of three seeds each by making shallow fingertip indentations in the compost. Place a seed in each hollow. Sieve ⅛ inch (5 mm) of soil over the surface, until the damp compost below just disappears. Again gently firm the surface with your palm – just a reassuring pat, the sort you'd give a nervous cat. Remember the shoots have to push their way up through the surface, so don't want too much of a struggle.

8 Write the date, name and number of seeds sown on the label; stick this into the edge of the container.

9 Cover the container with a plastic lid or some clingfilm, or put it into the electric propagator. When using a propagator, first spray its base, on which a little compost or sand has been laid, with water as this helps to create a Turkish-bath atmosphere. Place on a semi-sunny bedroom window sill where it will be looked at at least twice a day and won't suffer from neglect.

1^0 After a short time the walls and ceiling of the propagator or container cover will start to warm and pour with sweat. The tiny glow-worm light of a propagator-incubator switches itself on and off. Whether it is wishful thinking or just imagination, the bedroom feels different. There is a sense (particularly during the night) of something else being in the room. Even though the seeds are only miniscule in size, they are alive. You are not alone.

Types of parsley

Italian plain-leaved parsley (*Petroselinum crispum*) is not the only kind. There is also:
√ 'Champion Moss Curled'
√ French
√ Hamburg
√ 'Italian Giant'
√ Mitsuba (Japanese)
√ Neapolitan (*P. c.* var. *neapolitanum*)
√ 'Rina'

All have a different taste, appearance, colour and texture. Why not become a parsley specialist?

Cat-grass lawn

If for some reason you don't like parsley or are anxious about sowing seeds, you could, if you have a cat, grow a portable cat-grass lawn. These can be found (pre-sown) in boxes in pet shops and some supermarkets. Just add water. Each morning, before breakfast, my cats rush like health fanatics to their portable lawn and, heads turned sideways, chew down the stems, enjoying a pre-breakfast salad.

Other things to do in January

Go to the children's library and look for a book on seeds to find out what is actually inside those grey rowing-boat parsley seeds. Children's books are, on the whole, better illustrated than adults' and, on subjects like this, easier to understand. Within the seed coat lies a minuscule seed (the ovule of a plant), inside which is a tiny new plant consisting of a seed leaf, shoot and root (and a larder of food to live on).

Find out about wormeries, although it is still too cold to inaugurate one yet (see pages 30-33).

Potatoes can be grown in 8 inch (20 cm) pots, potato barrels and thick, black plastic bags. It is too late to order special ones now (order in October–November for delivery in December –March). This year have a trial potato growing, either with those that start sprouting of their own accord in the bottom of the refrigerator, or by buying seed potatoes from a garden centre.

Consider growing saffron (i.e. planting *Crocus sativus* corms). Read about saffron's long and interesting history (for a potted version and a description of a visit to a Spanish saffron festival, see pages 135-142).

Plan on starting a simple in-a-plastic-sack or plastic-dustbin compost heap (see pages 48-50).

Look out for unusual vegetables in greengrocers and supermarkets. Go to Chinese, Caribbean, Turkish and Indian greengrocers and buy vegetables you've never seen before and whose names you don't know. Choose those that have root-sprouting possibilities. Chinese single-clove garlic, lemongrass, sweet potatoes, Japanese artichokes: all these, and more, can be started off indoors in water or suspended just above it, with the base touching but not submerged (or it will rot). In the case of sweet potatoes, if one end doesn't root, simply turn it upside down and try the other.

Try to buy organic seeds (see pages 217-219) to stop the spread of non-germinating, terminator-gene seeds (those that are sterile – unlike the fertile profits of some seed companies, which force us to buy more and more seeds instead of saving them). Terminator-gene seeds must be one of the most dire combinations of mammonism and immorality – something that one imagines could only take place in science fiction.

The onset of spring

The days are getting lighter by a minute a day, or so says the weekend edition of *The Times*. The lid of darkness is being raised – fractionally – and with it our expectations. But this is still the time of year to tuck up in the warm poring over details of last year's triumphs and disasters. The following is a sample from a seed-sowing diary written last spring when growing tomatoes for the first time:

Day 1 A packet of tomato seeds: so light in weight there's no castanet-rattle when they're shaken. Yet these dust-sized specks (assisted by the four elements) contain potential stems, scent, leaves, pollen, colour, root and rootlets, taste, flesh, sap, flowers, texture, fruit, juice and yet more seeds for next year's harvest: they contain the future – something that should never be taken for granted. An electric propagator: it is seed-tray in size, attached by a cord to a plug, has a greenhouse-like top with ventilation slides and fits on a bedroom window sill. Compost: moist, warm-ish in its plastic sack and fine; I'd be perfectly content to germinate in this comfortable looking soil. Fingers are sifted through it – like making short-crust pastry. The tray is filled to the brim, levelled, then firmed down with a presser board, which resembles a

Day 1, contd wooden palm on the surface of the soil. A pinch of the fragile, fly-away seeds is scattered from above. If two or more seeds insist on lying together, they are coaxed apart – a fingertip away from each other. Between the palms, a 'rain' of ¼ inch (10 mm) of compost is sifted, then gently pressed down. Greenhouse cover is placed on top, 'electric blanket' switched on, propagator put on the window sill and the curtain a quarter drawn to shade the tray from too much light. This compost bed is made with more care than one makes one's own.

After sowing, the now-invisible seeds are left alone in their centrally heated indoor 'greenhouse'. It is a time to wait.

Wake up in the night to see if tiny orange thermostat light is on. Wonder what is silently and mysteriously taking place in the soil – or perhaps not so silently if one could really hear: the sound of seed cases splitting open.

Day 2, morning Greenhouse top is misted and sweating. Peer through the misting to see if anything is happening. It isn't – visibly.

Day 5, early morning	Faint eruptions have appeared on the soil surface, which could have been made by tentative moles.
Day 5, later in the day	Mole-eruptions have become larger and are now miniature earthquakes, as the thin-as-hair stems push upwards, heads still underground.
Day 5, evening	Heads are still buried, arched stems resembling croquet hoops on a lawn.
Day 5, midnight	Croquet hoops are no longer there. In only a few hours the heads have risen, breaking out of their seed coats and are now upright, two-leaved. What force is needed, first, to create the eruption upheavals in the compost and, second, to raise the fragile stems from horizontal to vertical?
Day 6, 6 am	Greenhouse top is removed. Seedlings lean away from the room towards the window, leaves outstretched horizontally like a troupe of gymnasts.
Day 6, 9 pm	Leaves raised upwards, folded together – like gymnasts exercising.

Day 7, morning   Turn tray round so that leaning-towards-the-light seedlings can straighten their stems.

Day 7, evening   All stems are straight. After a few more window sill days in the sun – with the curtain protecting them at night from the open window's air – it is time for them to go outside. First into a miniature outdoor 'greenhouse' (i.e. a large plastic cloche), but only for the choicest slice of the day – its middle. Then back they come in the late afternoon.

In and out they go each morning and evening. All of the seed packet's promised contents have germinated. All thirty stems are now protected by the finest, fur-like hairs – vertical halos when seen against the light. Only a few are late beginners, handicapped by seed cases that remain clamped to their two leaves, preventing them from opening. It is tempting to assist and release them, but more interesting to resist and see how the struggling leaves manage to free themselves.

It is time to do a little judicious thinning-out of seedlings that are grow-

Day 7, evening contd

ing too close together, endangering each other. Now's the moment to test whether they already smell or taste of tomato. They don't, neither stem nor leaves. But then the shape of the first two seed leaves gives no hint of what they are going to become – unlike basil at the same age. Long before basil seedlings are 'large enough to handle', they are imbued with the cloveish spiciness of their future.

Day 11

Third leaf is preparing to appear. It is triple-, not single-, lobed even in infancy, and this is the first sign of the tomato plant it is going to become. Does this visual indication also hold the identifying smell and taste? No. Still it releases no scent.

Day 12

Although the tomato plants are still too fragile to be watered from above, even with a fine rose spray, they are now sturdy enough to stand up for themselves against breezes, trembling only slightly without toppling over. Watering is done with the narrowest watering-can spout, dribbled on to

Day 12, compost in which desert-like cracks
contd appear.

Seed sowing must be one of the
most absorbing of occupations. It is not
only the actual doing of it, but also the
anticipation, the anxieties and thoughts
surrounding it... imagining what is
going on *inside* the seed tray, as the
white galaxy of fragile roots spreads
through the dark earth.

Rush back early from a party to
close the window and rescue the
tomato plants from an unexpected drop
in temperature.

Day 18 Pricking-out day – the move from tray
to individual pots. Fill 3½ inch (9 cm)
pots with compost. Use both thumbs to
make a hole in the centre – like making
a clay pinch-pot – to receive the plant
and its roots. Scoop out a heaped
dessertspoonful of chocolate-coloured
cake compost in the centre of which is a
small, giraffe-like creature with its long,
furry neck-stem and white spider's-web
roots. Place in the hole.

One by one the pots line up. Glance
down and notice that the first of the

Day 18 contd transplants is drooping; prop it up with a pea-size piece of compost. Only a few minutes later, in the time it took to make a cup of coffee, panic! Fifteen plants are drooping – sulking in unison. Race at ambulance speed to place the fifteen casualties ankle-deep in a trough of water.

Wait for the first signs of recovery, and discover the compost bag's planting instructions: the pots should have been watered before, not after, pricking-out. It is touch and go.

After what seems a long time, but is in fact short for stems and leaves to rise from facing the earth to facing the sky, the panic is over.

First whole night in 'greenhouse'.

Day 19 Raise cloche to see how plants have fared in their pots. All are flourishing.

Day 22 Fifth leaf appearing. Plants are now stocky enough to be watered from above with a fine rose spray. Stems are thickening. Fur-like stem hairs stop at the two first leaves, then the fur thins out, becoming more hair-like – fine barbed wire to deter insects perhaps.

Day 25   Three-lobed leaves are now resilient
          enough for raindrops to balance and
          perch without toppling them. When all
          twenty-nine plants are flourishing with
          four or five leaves, the last of the late-
          beginner's first two leaves still remain
          clasped together, forcing the growing
          tip sideways; despite this stubbornness,
          the third and fourth leaves have
          managed to open.

Day 25   At last, by bending low over the tomato
          plants, it is possible to smell their
          peppery scent that they keep close to
          themselves. Soon gangly adolescent
          stems will need cane supports. The rest
          of the tomato story is known.

Seeds to sow now (indoors)

√ Italian flat-leaved parsley (*Petroselinum crispum*)
√ 'Gardeners' Delight' tomatoes (*Lycopersicon esculentum*)
  (January–March, says the packet)
√ Sweet peas (*Lathyrus odoratus*) (January–mid-May)

What to eat now

Fried parsley: an alternative to croutons

Why did fried parsley become unfashionable, to be replaced by fried seaweed which is generally not seaweed but cabbage?

2 large handfuls of parsley
corn oil (or other mild-flavoured oil)

Remove the lower, thicker stems from two large handfuls of what is now imaginatively called 'bunched parsley' (i.e. 'Champion Moss Curled' parsley). Wash thoroughly. Drain and dry even more thoroughly. In a wok heat about an inch of corn oil until very hot. When a test piece of parsley sizzles and rises to the top when placed in the oil, the rest is ready to be put in. Fry until crisp and dark green. Remove with a slotted spoon and drain on several sheets of absorbent paper.

FEBRUARY

A riddle

Question: What creature has no eyes, ears, nose, teeth, arms or legs? Yet this creature has five hearts; it moves, eats, breathes through its skin, has senses, is both male and female, mates – with both male and females – can live for fifteen years or longer, never sleeps and makes new earth.

Answer: An earthworm.

With their constant munching and mating (with not only the opposite, but their own, sex), breeding, producing of vermi-compost and lack of sleep, what exhausting lives worms live.

There are not a lot of gardening activities at this time of the year, so now would be a good moment to consider making or buying a wormery and producing worm casts (i.e. worm manure).

Window sill wormeries

Wormeries are ideal for window-box gardens: a) because they are small, b) because they can, if necessary, be kept indoors, c) because the worms require only small amounts of food, and, d) because a working wormery is a most interesting procedure to watch.

Some people can't even bear to hear the word 'worm' said aloud, let alone whispered. But after reading about the intriguing life of a worm and being introduced to them gradually – perhaps to a baby worm first, and then to the head end of an adolescent – even anti-wormers might overcome their aversion. It would be worth it.

Worms have enthusiastic appetites and eat their way through half their own body weight in food each day. Because they have special digestive systems, the results of their banqueting – worm casts (the earth that is excreted by worms) – are much richer in nutrients than the original food. Worm-cast compost can be mixed with existing soil when refreshing window boxes in the spring (see pages 52-3), used as a slow-release top-dressing, or as an alternative to peat. (If, when in Ireland, you have ever seen peat being machine-dug from the body of the land, you will probably never use it again.)

You can make your own wooden wormery (both the Henry Doubleday Research Association and Chase Organics provide instructions, see pages 217-19), buy one or enquire whether your local council will give you one free (or at a reduced rate), this being the councils' attempts to encourage people to recycle and cut down on the landfill-waste problem. This is an excellent council initiative but has its drawbacks: I've tried two council plastic wormeries and neither worked, the result in both cases being a swamp at the bottom of the bins from which the worms, quite understandably, were constantly trying to escape. I also bought what appeared to be an airier version of the council's wormery. Result: third swamp. Conclusion: worms don't like living in airless plastic containers – who would? I've yet to meet a worm-composter who has had any success with plastic – or at least with this particular design. I'm sorry for those people who have given up worm-composting due to failure, because wormeries *can* work.

The most successful wormery I have had was called a Tiger Worm Compost Bin and was made of recycled newspapers and cardboard (see pages 217-19). It allowed air to enter and excess moisture to leave and evaporate. Owing to its composition, it won't last for ever, though mine endured for several years. At the moment I'm experimenting with what might, or might not, turn out to be the simplest and cheapest design of all (see page 128-9).

In the meantime, while making your own wormery or waiting for an ordered one to arrive, here are a few worm 'biographical' details.

The species generally used for vermicomposting are the red worm (*Eisenia andreii*) or the tiger worm (*Eisenia foetida*), so called because of its dark reddish colour and buff stripes. The reds and tigers are not from the same family as common earthworms (*Lumbricus terrestris*), which live deeper down in the earth and do different work, burrowing and aerating the soil. Reds and tigers live in the organic mulch on the earth's surface and spend most of their time eating and producing nutrients for the soil. Without worms there would be no plants or trees.

> *"Earthworms are the intenstines of the earth."*
> Aristotle (381–322 BC)

Worm myth – one of the questions frequently asked about worms is: if they are cut in two, do they grow another head and rear? No. This is just one of those stories we like and seem to need to keep, but is as far from the truth as the story about bats being blind vampires and having a fondness for entangling themselves in people's hair. However, sometimes the head end of a cut-in-half worm will survive.

Parsley check no. 1

By now the results of the trial parsley-seed sowing should be making an appearance. Keep a watchful eye on what is happening beneath the steamy propagator lid, but don't lift and peep too often. This lowers the temperature, reduces the claustrophobic, tropical atmosphere – and is intrusive.

After a week, more or less (each seed is different), specks of bright greenness will be seen against the dark compost. A day or so later the specks will rise, their fragile stems finer than babies' hair. Some seedlings emerge still 'wearing' their hat-like seed coats. As hour by hour they grow taller, open the propagator vents to let in a little outside-world air.

When the majority have made their début (another advantage of counting them while sowing), it is time to move them from the intensive care of the propagator-incubator to the less sheltered maternity ward of the window sill, with its changing temperatures, air currents and direct sunlight. Place the container on top of the propagator lid, where there may be some remnants of warmth.

⚘

Studying seed catalogues

Now is the time to start looking through seed catalogues, a most pleasurable winter-evening-by-lamplight occupation. Just seeing the pictures and reading the descriptions – of sugar snap peas and night-scented stock – makes summer leap out of the February darkness. What is almost unimaginable when sitting in front of a fire on a dark winter's evening – open windows, endless summer days, languorous evenings – suddenly becomes imaginable.

Here is a list of vegetables (just some of them), herbs, scented plants, and a spice that can be grown in window boxes and pots:

√ Abyssinian mustard (also known by the less beguiling name of Texsel greens). A recently introduced brassica, with glossy leaves and a spinach flavour.

√ Alpine strawberry (*Fragaria alpina*)

√ Aubergine (*Solanum melongena*)

√ Basil (*Ocimum basilicum*)

√ Beans, dwarf or French (*Phaseolus vulgaris*) and runner (*Phaseolus coccineus*)

√ Beetroot (*Beta vulgaris*) 'Detroit 2-Tardel'

√ Chicory (*Cichorium intybus*) – use young leaves for salads

√ Chinese cabbage (*Brassica rapa* Chinensis Group)

√ Chives (*Allium schoenoprasum*)

√ Cress, American Land (*Lepidium sativum*, also called Belle Isle cress, early winter cress and upland cress). Remains green all winter, can be used instead of watercress.

√ Cucumber (*Cucumis sativa*)

√ Dill (*Anethum graveolens*)

√ Garlic (*Allium sativum*)

√ Garlic chives

√ Komatsuna (also called mustard spinach). Japanese, but related to the turnip, use it in salads – or wait a little longer and stir-fry.

√ Lamb's lettuce (*Valeriana locusta*, also called corn salad and mâche)

√ Lettuce (*Lactuca sativa*), 'Salad Bowl' and 'Black Seeded Simpson'

√ Mignonette – for its scent.

√ Mitsuba (also called Japanese parsley). The seeds are slim and dark jade green – not surprising considering its nationality – with vertical stripes. Has an Angelica taste.

√ Mizuna (also called potherb mustard). Japanese. Juicy – can be cooked or used in salads.

√ Nasturtiums (*Tropaeolaceae majus*)
√ Night-scented stock (*Matthiola bicornis*)
√ Oriental saladini – a mixture of oriental salads
√ Pak choi – can be eaten as a salad
√ Parsley (*Petroselinum crispum*)
√ Peas (*Pisum sativum*), mange-tout and sugar-snap
√ Perpetual spinach
√ Potatoes (*Solanum tuberosum*)
√ Radish (*Raphanus sativus*)
√ Rocket (*Eruca sativa*)
√ Saffron (*Crocus sativus*)
√ Scarole – use in salads
√ Spinach (*Spinacia oleracea*)
√ Sweet peppers (*Capsicum annuum* Grassum Group)
√ Swiss chard (*Beta vulgaris* Cicla Group)
√ Tomatoes (*Lycopersicon esculentum*)
√ Vegetable amaranth – use in salads or stir-fries
√ Winter purslane (also called miner's lettuce, Indian lettuce, Claytonia). Has heart-shaped succulent leaves, use in salads.

Window-box gardening is more suited, on the whole, to cut-and-come-again vegetables, such as 'Salad Bowl' lettuce, Swiss chard and perpetual spinach, which continually replenish themselves throughout their growing season. A single 'Tom Thumb' lettuce is cut once – and that's that until the next one is sown.

Resist the temptation to buy too many plants or seeds. They all need attention, but not fragmented or diluted attention, under which they will not thrive – and neither will the sower. Growing seeds is like travelling, in that it is better to see more of less, than less of more. Your concentration acts like a fertiliser – just as it does on both humans and animals. If you stroke a person or an animal while reading or listening to the radio, your hand feels empty and automatic. Animals are particularly aware of this and, quite rightly, object. You have to remember what you are doing when sowing seeds: you are helping to perform a miracle. That something the size of a speck of dust, which can be blown away by a breeze, sneeze or sigh, needs only to be placed in or on soil to germinate *is* miraculous.

There are vegetables to match the whole spectrum of colour, apart from blue. So why is blue excluded, reserved for flowers and sky?

And how undemanding vegetables are. They will flourish in fields, suspended in mid-air in hanging baskets, in greenhouses, pots, pans, allotments, potagers, on roof gardens and terraces.

Planting an orchard

Even if you have only a very small, sunny balcony or roof garden there is still room to include an orchard, or at least one miniature, self-fertile fruit tree (see pages 217-19). My roof garden has a 'Comice' and a 'Conference' pear, a 'Victoria' plum and a 'Sunburst' cherry, all comfortably growing in 14 x 14 x 12 inch (36 x 36 x 30 cm) tubs. At least they're sufficiently comfortable to produce fruit, despite the cherry and plum being self-fertile – rather a lonely occupation.

Now is the time to order an 'orchard'. Trees can be planted between November and April and generally arrive with simple planting instructions.

Ordering saffron corms

Mid-February is also the time to order saffron (*Crocus sativus*) corms (see pages 217-19) for planting between June and August. It is important to buy *C. sativus* and not sub-species or *C. speciosus*, which is what a lot of the so-called *C. sativus* corms are.

Chitting potatoes

This means placing potatoes in an egg box and leaving them in a cool place to enable them to start sprouting (chitting) in time for planting in April

Parsley check no. 2

After only a few hours on the window sill, the seedling stems will have straightened. When the sun reaches them, all members of the ensemble will lean towards it. Keep turning their tray clockwise (clockwise because it is easier to remember), so that all sides receive equal light. If seedlings respond in this way to the sun, do they respond nocturnally, too, to the moon? Some gardeners believe so and sow at night. If the moon can change people's moods and pull tides along, why not seeds out of their cases?

Scented congregation

Although my 'allotment' consists mainly of vegetables, it was formerly a scented roof garden, so naturally there are still a few members of the scented congregation left, such as Persian lilac, *Wisteria sinensis*, vanilla-scented *Clematis montana*, *Rosa* 'Zéphirine Drouhin', freesias, a portable indoor-outdoor orange bush, *Viburnum* x *buckwoodii*, lavender for lavender bags and *Lilium regale*, which have been living contentedly in the same 8 inch (20 cm) pots for many years. There are also three different honeysuckles, two different jasmines and *Trachelospermum* 'Japonicum', which specialises in autumns, having two each year – the first a private one in spring, when the leaves turn bright red, and the second with all the other plants in autumn, when the leaves again become red.

Apart from the residents mentioned above, night-scented stock (which must be one of the smallest flowers to produce such a huge scent) can also be grown. It doesn't object to being brought indoors for the evening to scent a room. Also sweet peas and mignonette, that old-fashioned-looking, grandmotherly plant. If a choice had to be made between vegetables, fruit, scented plants and plants for colour, I'd put them in the above order.

For brilliance and cheerfulness there is the confetti-like Virginia stock, nasturtiums and *Impatiens*, the last because of their clashing pink-reds and because they are supposed to be difficult to grow (or at least the F1 hybrid is). Their germination boosts horticultural confidence.

However, growing solely vegetables need not result in a colourless garden. There are red and white bean flowers, yellow cucumber flowers, purple aubergine flowers, beige rocket flowers, pale yellow pak choi flowers and white basil flowers, to mention just a few.

Parsley check no. 3

After a short time the first two seedling leaves will unclasp each other and stretch out horizontally. When they are all out-stretched, there will be very little standing room in the seed tray. Possibly a few other seeds (generally known as weeds) will also have enjoyed the incubation period. Remove them and any weak or overcrowded parsley seedlings. This can be done either with agile fingertips or with tweezers.

Don't discard the parsley seedlings – eat them. These slim, elongated leaves are unidentifiable as parsley (it is the third leaf that reveals what the plant is), except in their taste, which could be nothing else but parsley. It is astonishing that some-thing so diminutive, which is just a few days old and has only a stem and two leaves, can be filled with its own unmistakable taste, many times more pungent than its size, but occupying only a minute portion of the mouth.

Germination summary

✓ Sown January 28th
✓ First appearance February 6th
✓ First two leaves February 19th
✓ Third leaf revealed February 21st. This is the minute, trifoliate leaf that announces what the plant is: not dill, alpine strawberry or basil (these look completely different), but Italian plain-leaved parsley.

Apart from all-year-round parsley, and possibly tomatoes, there are a few other seeds that can be sown this month, though don't be tempted to do this too early. Seedlings don't like the cold, or standing around on a window sill becoming leggy before being taken outside. Those who live on the Shetland Islands will start sowing later than those on the Scilly Isles.

Seeds to sow now (indoors)

✓ Garlic chives (February–April)
✓ Basil 'Bush' (*Ocimum basilicum*) (February–April)
✓ Basil 'Sweet Green' (*Ocimum basilicum*) (February–April)
✓ Alpine strawberry (*Fragaria alpina*) (February)
✓ Busy Lizzies (*Impatiens walleriana*) (mid-February–April)

What to eat now

Ten-minute Roman bread

This recipe is a good way to exercise hands in preparation for all the work they will be doing during the following months in the allotment. It is called Ten-minute Roman bread because this is the time it takes to weigh out the ingredients, mix, knead and leave to rise. The rest of the work – rising and baking – is done by the oven.

1 lb (450 g) organic Spelt flour (*Triticum spelta*, an ancient precursor of modern wheat varieties)
1 x 2½ oz (70g) sachet Easy-Bake or Fast-Action yeast
1 tsp (5 ml) sea salt
1 tbsp (15 ml) sunflower or olive oil
425ml (¾ pint) warm water – ¼ pint or 150 ml of boiling water from the kettle, the rest from the cold tap; this mixture gives just the right temperature

Preheat the oven to 190°C/375°F/Gas mark 5. Oil a baking tray measuring approximately 13 x 9 inches (33 x 23 cm). Place the flour, yeast, salt and oil in a large bowl. Mix gently. Add water bit by bit while stirring with your hand. Some flours are 'thirstier' than others. When the dough ball leaves the sides of the bowl, turn onto a flat surface and knead until the dough feels springy. Form into a ball – or any other shape you like. Place in the centre of the tray. Cover with a clean cloth and leave to rise in a warm place (i.e. near the oven). The rising will take 30–45 minutes. Bake in the pre-heated oven on a middle shelf for 30–35 minutes. A cooked loaf will sound hollow when tapped underneath. Cool the loaf on a wire rack. Resist slicing the bread until it is completely cold.

Variations

You can try using different millers' flours; using half white half brown, all white, or all brown flour, adding rye flour, cornmeal or other grains. A whole variety of seeds, nuts and fruits can be included when mixing the dough. These include: poppy seeds (black and white), pumpkin seeds (with or without a tamari coating), sesame seeds, sunflower seeds, sunflower hearts, hazelnuts, pinenuts, almonds, walnuts, brazils, raisins, currants, sultanas and olives (black and green). Nuts and seeds can be toasted or untoasted. A generous handful or two will be sufficient.

The surface of the loaf can be left bare or, just before it is put into the oven, sprinkled with flour and painted with egg yolk or white. The surface can also be quickly and gently wetted with warm water – just sufficient to make seeds or grains stick. It can then be sprinkled with sesame seeds, poppy seeds, polenta, soaked wheat grains, cracked wheat or golden linseed.

Parsley check no. 4

As soon as the parsley seedlings have developed their first two true leaves, it is time to prick them out into more spacious individual accommodation. This can be obtained in various forms: recycled plastic modules (i.e. child-sized yoghurt pots), bio-degradable plant trays or containers made from old news-papers using a Pot Maker (see pages 217-19). This is a minute wooden press (which would also be suitable for making fezzes for Egyptian dolls). No glue or skill is required and the news-paper eventually blends into the soil after the seedling has been transplanted.

If using pre-punched plastic modules, make certain that the drainage hole has been properly punched, otherwise the module will become waterlogged: would you like to live in a bog? Half-fill the individual containers with compost, making a small hollow to receive the seedling. With a teaspoon, gently scoop out a plant from the original container, taking care not to hurt the roots; they have been just as busy under-ground as the stem and leaf have been above.

Don't hold the plant by its stem – this is the most delicate part; holding it here is the equivalent of someone being hoisted up by the neck. If the seedling must be touched, hold the leaves carefully and, with forefinger and thumb (which suddenly feel gigantic and Gulliverish), gently place the lilliputian seedling in the centre of its new container. Add more soil until this nearly reaches the top, allowing for it to swell when watered. Gently press down the compost, making certain that the stem is straight and the seedling looks secure and comfortable.

An alternative to the teaspoon method is to break the seed-tray contents carefully into single seedling portions, as though breaking a crumbly cake. This probably does less damage to the roots.

> *"The lilliput, countless armies of the grass."*
> WALT WHITMAN (1819–92), LEAVES OF GRASS

This part of gardening must surely bring out the maternal and paternal in the most un-motherly or un-fatherly of gardeners.

Pricking-out and transplanting are such intimate, gentle and peaceful occupations that they are better performed in silence, the ears unclogged by so-called background music or talk, which fills the foreground and induces a fuzzy semi-listening, semi-seeing state.

As the pricking-out of all the other seedlings continues, the window ledge will soon become too small in its new capacity as seedling kindergarten. On either side of my bedroom window frame are two permanent brackets, on to which each spring I put a removable shelf to accommodate all the additional pots. If plastic modules are being used, they can be cut to the width of the shelf. After a time it is difficult to see out of the window, but this doesn't matter for the few weeks during which there is so much to see inside.

Although my flat has central heating, the bedroom radiator is turned off during the propagation season, because it becomes too hot for the seeds and seedlings. This leaves the bedroom on the chilly side, so I now resort to a small electric fire, placed as far away as possible from the window.

The survivors

Something else to check is last year's late autumnal sowings. After almost disappearing during the most severe months, mitsuba, claytonia, lamb's lettuce, American land cress, rocket and winter purslane reappear – small and bright green, as though they've been on holiday rather than undergoing the endurance test of winter.

The making of compost

The making of compost (though a less extreme version than that quoted below), as opposed to worm compost, is not only for garden gardeners. To begin, all that is needed is a container with a lid, large enough to store a week's supply of what is inaccurately called 'kitchen waste'.

"Martyrs' ashes are the best compost to manure the church."
THOMAS FULLER (1608–61), THE HISTORY OF THE HOLY WAR

March is a good time to start because it is the month that contains the vernal equinox and heralds the gradual lengthening of the days, making going outside more inviting.

Instead of throwing away potato peel, citrus rind, dead flowers, tea leaves and tea bags – plus all the other detritus that is put into the rubbish bin – use them to replenish and enrich the soil. For those with a well-developed Scrooge-ish side, this particular form of thrift should be especially appealing. Anything that has been alive can be used, though it is advisable not to add the remains of animal and fish corpses, as these can attract flies.

Roughly chop up banana skins and so on, as though making a very chunky salad for a very large animal, and put them into the container. This chopping-up might seem a nuisance at first, but isn't really (especially when you think of the landfill-sites-versus-compost debate) and soon becomes a habit.

Composting begins in the container, when the 'salad' starts to ferment, lose its individuality, release its water content, reduce slightly in volume and, mysteriously, become faintly warm as it commences its return to the earth from where it came. It is a sort of ashes-to-ashes process, a metamorphosis in reverse. Some people may find it unappealing, but if you know what is happening and observe it, it becomes interesting.

When the container is full, a large, sturdy, plastic garden-waste sack will be needed with ready-made ventilation holes; alternatively the holes can be made with a paper hole-puncher, or a ready-made bag called Compost-a-Cube, can be bought (see pages 217-19).

Transfer the contents of the container to the plastic sack.

Loosely secure the top and continue the squirreling-away procedure in the container.

Each time more material is added to the sack, mix everything together. Probably the mixing of compost by hand isn't everyone's cup of tea, but there is nothing really unpleasant about it; in fact, it is most interesting if you remember what the ingredients were, and are now becoming. For those who don't like the idea of touching compost – it is only the idea – wear gloves (see the anti-glove lecture on page 13.) Garages supply free plastic gloves that, probably unbeknown to them, are ideal for this purpose. However, it is more interesting to feel the material on your skin. Remind yourself that you are adding to the earth, without which there would be nowhere for us to stand.

What is soil?

The inauguration of my first compost heap (before graduating to the sack) took place in a plastic dustbin, which has a lid that can be secured by two clasps. When the lid was 'locked' and the bin rolled sideways and turned upside down and downside up, it acted like one of the more superior tumbler compost bins. Eventually it became too full, heavy and stuffy, and I moved on to the sack. Nevertheless, it was quite useful for the initial stage.

"Soil is the breathing skin of the earth."
ANON.

For those who have friends with lawns, ask for a small bag of mowings. Or get to know a public or private park gardener. Mowed grass creates heat, but if too much is added it clogs up the compost and makes it lumpy. Always sprinkle it on, don't just dump it. Then mix well. What is this mysterious heat? What creates it? Mainly bacteria. As they work away, breaking down the organic material, their energy is released in the form of heat.

Straw is another ingredient that compost likes and which helps aerate it, but as bails of straw are not usually synonymous with towns, torn-up newspaper may be used instead. Compost does not, however, like shiny *Radio Times* sort of paper.

Add dead plants from the allotment, too, but cut them up. Don't add woody stems or leaves. Leaf-composting is quite another branch of compost-making, but only for the patient and young as it can take several years for leaves to turn into mould.

Each weekend open the sack to give it fresh air, and mix it up. After only a few weeks everything will start to sink, become heavier, wetter, darker and unrecognisable, like a very organic hippopotamus-portion of muesli. It is still a long way from being compost, yet an equally long way from banana skins and tea leaves. It is now somewhere in between. Fruit flies may visit it, but they're harmless.

One of the main concerns of amateur compost makers is: does it smell? This depends on your nose, and although compost could never be mistaken for Chanel No. 5, there is nothing unpleasant about it. What is more unpleasant is today's obsession (when concerned with compost) with everything having to be odour-free. How bleak an odour-free world would be.

Preparing window boxes and pots for sowing

March is the month for the first-time window-box gardener to buy window boxes and pots. Unless there is room for only one window box, don't buy anything too big. About 27 x 8 x 8 inches (70 x 20 x 20 cm) is a good size, because even when it is full of earth and plants, and watered, it is still liftable.

Buy organic compost – not the one for seed-sowing, but the more adult version for transplanting and planting. It will only have to be bought once if you have a compost sack and wormery. Put concave crocks (broken flower pots) over the drainage holes in the window box to allow any water to drain away. Then fill with compost.

If window boxes and pots are already available, remove about 1 inch (2.5 cm) of the tired topsoil (this can be added to the compost sack), empty out the rest and sift through it to remove any old roots and lumps. Add a child's handful of pelletised chicken manure, which resembles dry breakfast cereal, or, better still, use the above with added seaweed – available from some nurseries, garden centres and organic suppliers (see pages 217-19). If compost and/or worm manure has already been made, mix in several large handfuls. This mixture should supply most of the nourishment the plants will need, though later in the year liquid seaweed can be applied, or used as a foliar feed. Don't be too generous with the fertiliser; this results in horticultural indigestion. Return the refreshed soil to the boxes and pots. Water – but don't flood them and create a bog.

My window boxes are divided into three horizontal 'plots', according to the height and habit of the vegetables: for example, tomatoes in the back row, dwarf or French beans in the middle and cut-and-come-again lettuce (or rocket) in the front stalls.

Sowing in a window box

Take a support cane that is just a bit shorter than the length of the box. Place it on the compost, about 1 inch (2.5 cm) from the edge, and create a furrow to the depth suggested on the seed packet, by pressing the cane down and moving it to and fro sideways, making certain that the soil on either side of the furrow is roughly the same in amount (this will be used for covering the seeds). Place a pinch of seeds in your clean palm and sprinkle sparingly into furrow. Cover with soil made by the furrowing action. Write the date and the name of the seeds on a label – otherwise you will forget.

Some of the larger seeds, like the wrinkled worried-looking spinach and the seahorse-tail segments of chard, can be sown individually. Ignore the packet's instructions and sow close together, about 3 inches (7.5 cm) apart, not 8 inches (20 cm) – there isn't the space to spare and they don't seem to mind living close together. Sow a couple more, just in case any fail to germinate.

With the larger seeds, count how many you have sown and add this to the label information. Sometimes six are put in, and up pop eight. With the smaller sprinklable seeds, don't sow too many. You don't want a glut of vegetables. Though the word 'glut' when linked to containers may seem a slight exaggeration, it is not. I've had 'gluts' of tomatoes (despite giving them away to friends and puréeing and freezing them), beans, lettuce and basil. It is better to sow little and often.

Sowing tip: medium-sized seeds (those too small for lifting with finger-and-thumb) can be sown individually by taking a light-coloured pencil, licking the tip, then lifting the seed by the dampened tip and transferring it to the compost.

Worm menu

If a wormery has been ordered, the worms' accommodation will arrive first by parcel post, giving time to follow the instructions and set it up for the tenants, who will arrive a few days later by letter post. Worms are not generally posted on Fridays, to avoid having them loitering in sorting offices over the weekend.

While waiting for their arrival, start collecting food; they only need a snack at this stage. Compost heaps and wormeries require different 'diets'. This doesn't mean that you have to open a canteen and cater specially for the reds and tigers. They like apple peel, bread, banana skins, baked beans, cabbage stalks and outer leaves, old cake, coffee grounds, outer celery stalks, old cheese, cucumber tops and bottoms, torn-up newspapers, eggshells, egg and milk cartons (soaked first), cold porridge, pasta, pineapple skin, cooked potatoes, plate scrapings, tea leaves and tea bags. They don't like the peel of lemons, limes or oranges or onion skins, which are too acid. They hate nappy liners, grass and cat or dog faeces. As they have no teeth, they prefer to have their food cut up small.

From now on, instead of throwing away eggshells and all the other 'menu' items listed above, start collecting them. The eggshells can be dried in an oven – or let the air do the drying and then grind them up.

Why do worms need eggshells? Because they have no teeth, food is ground down in their gizzards. Grains of sand and mineral particles collect in the gizzard, the muscular walls of which contract, compressing the hard particles and food while mixing it with digestive juices and grinding it down. Birds' gizzards work in a similar way, and so do waste-disposal units; did their inventors copy the worms – or birds?

Eggshells provide grit and calcium carbonate, which is necessary for reproduction and to prevent the wormery from becoming too acid. Powdered limestone, which does the same job, can be used instead. But eggshells are free, where limestone is not, and when using the latter you miss out on the collecting, drying and grinding process which makes you more a part of the wormery process – an aspect some would perhaps be prepared to sacrifice.

Worms' arrival

When the worms arrive they should be placed in the wormery immediately and allowed to recover from their journey. Don't peep at them, they don't like light and need a little privacy.

Parsley check no. 5

As soon as the March air becomes a little warmer and the sun a little stronger, the four-leaved parsley seedlings can be taken for a visit to the outside world – like putting a baby out in its pram for the first time. Before it gets dark, bring in the seedlings. Repeat these 'acclimatisation' outings each sunny day.

The first time I (unsuccessfully) grew melons, I took great care to follow my own advice, to the extent that I had to rush home early from a party, suddenly having remembered the stranded melon seedlings freezing to death outdoors.

Arrival of ordered seeds

By now the ordered seeds should have arrived by letter post. If all the produce they will produce were to be returned – the total harvest of stems, shoots, flowers and fruit – a small van would probably be needed.

The sound of them rattling like small maracas in their slim packets fills one with expectation.

seeds to sow now (indoors)

√ Aubergine (*Solanum melongena*) 'Slim Jim'

seed to sow now (outdoors)

√ Lettuce (*Lactuca sativa*), green and red 'Salad Bowl'
√ Perpetual spinach (a member of the beetroot family)
√ Spinach (*Spinacia oleracea*) 'New Zealand'
√ Swiss chard (*Beta vulgaris* Cicla Group) 'Jacob's Coat' (a
  member of the beetroot family)
√ Mignonette
√ Nasturtium (*Tropaeolum majus*)
√ Night-scented stock (*Matthiola bicornis*)
√ Virginia stock (*Matthiola incana*) with its minute
  cinnamon-coloured seed

Some of these seeds (for instance 'New Zealand' spinach and
Swiss chard) can also be sown in the autumn when sowing
possibilities are more limited. Depending on how much space
there is, it may be advisable to keep some of the autumnal
germinators until then, though chard in its rainbow version
(sometimes called 'Jacob's Coat', 'Rainbow Chard' or 'Bright
Lights') is so appealing that it is worth sowing in both spring
and autumn.

The stems and leaf-veins of chard may either be red,
yellow, burgundy, cream or white, the colour almost phos-
phorescent, appearing to be illuminated from within, seeping

up from below. The leaves may only be small and some are a little tough in the early part of the year. This is not surprising, since they have had to combat rain, wind, cold, ice and snow. But they provide a steamed salad that most rabbits would envy, even without a trickling of sesame oil and rice vinegar. Alternatively, instead of being turned into a salad, they can be dropped into simmering vegetable stock. As the year progresses and the weather relents, the plants do likewise and relax, producing a new, tender leaf crop.

What to eat now

steamed swiss chard salad

If leaves are big, cut stems into 1 inch (2.5 cm) lengths and place on a steamer rack. Cover with leaves. Steam until wilted. Chard is so full of taste and juice that it is delicious eaten as it is, undressed. If this does not appeal, add, while still warm, a trickle of olive, sesame or sunflower oil and either lemon, balsalmic or rice vinegar. Eat warm or cold.

Early-morning inspection

This is a most beneficial activity. Before starting work, go on a 'tour' of all the window boxes, tubs and pots and see what has happened since you last looked. It is not only us who are busy. New developments take place during the day and night: two leaves have suddenly become three. The bent-over stems of chives are straightening, their tips still weighed down by minute seed coats. Nasturtiums' furled-umbrella leaves are opening. In profile, the sweet peas now resemble meerkats. Tomato stems are furrier, their 'haloes' thickening. The cucumber's third leaf has serrated saw-tooth edges.

It is surely better for the eyes to see and be nourished by these sights than by half-digested horror headlines in the newspapers – that can come later. So can another inspection.

Revisiting the wormery

By now the worms will have settled down and be munching, mating, producing eggs, worm casts (manure) and liquid manure. The best moment to see them is at feeding time, when the lid is lifted and they are caught unawares: tunnelling through bean-pod interiors, massed together in a worm scrum, gambolling, turning somersaults and being generally playful... until they sense the light and within seconds have disappeared, gliding down beneath the compost's surface. A worm's whole body can taste and feel both light and sound. What do light and sound taste and feel like? Are they cool or warm, sweet or savoury? Sometimes, after heavy rain, a few of the younger worms may be found wandering around the lid area. If gently lifted, potential escapees can be returned to the clan. It is surprising how lively they can be, wriggling and squirming like the most wilful child – and all without arms or legs.

"So I went into the garden and ate three worms, two smooth ones and a hairy one; the hairy one tickled all the way down."
HILAIRE BELLOC (1870–1953)

They can also be quite skittish and coy at times, playing hide-and-seek by popping up and down out of the compost. A lot of life goes on beneath a wormery lid.

"A round little worm
Pricked from the lazy finger of a maid."
WILLIAM SHAKESPEARE (1564–1616), ROMEO AND JULIET

Idle worms: it was once supposed that little worms were bred in the fingers of idle servants.

Reproduction

As worms are hermaphrodites they have both ovaries and testes and during reproduction produce both eggs and sperm to fertilise the eggs. When mating, they lie side by side, facing in opposite directions, joined by a mucus-like substance that is produced by the clitellum. (This is the swollen band, sometimes called the 'saddle' or 'girdle', like a plump pink wedding ring, situated on the thirteenth segment about one-third of the distance between head and tail. It is quite easy to see and indicates that the worm is sexually mature.) Sperm passes from worm to worm. Later, a cocoon forms in the clitellum of each worm. Before the cocoons harden, the worms wriggle out backwards. As they do so, sperm and eggs are deposited in the cocoons as they pass over the openings of the ovaries and sperm storage sacs. When the cocoons are released from the worms (they drop off the ends, where the worms' 'noses' should be) they close up at both ends and egg fertilisation takes place inside. A worm cocoon is about the size of a grain of wheat, lemon-shaped, a translucent yellow-green in colour and could be mistaken for a tomato pip.

After a couple of weeks one or two baby worms will hatch from one end of the cocoon. After a year the babies will be fully grown.

Planting beans

This is the time for sowing one of the most dramatic of germinators: beans. Dwarf or French beans can be sown outside in May and runners from May to June, but they can also be sown inside now, where they can be observed more closely.

Either plant runner beans in saved-up toilet-roll interiors

or in a deepish (3 inch or 7.5 cm at least) saved-up plastic container. Make a hole with your finger, about 1½ inches (4 cm) deep (see the packet instructions), and place the bean inside, with its scar facing downwards. This is the point from which the root emerges. If placed the right way up (or, rather, down) to begin with, it saves the bean from having to swivel round.

Hanging baskets

As well as window boxes, pots and tubs, hanging baskets also make good receptacles for vegetables. Don't line them with that hideous, faded green padded-plastic or the equally unattractive and quickly disintegrating carpet-underlay or old doormat fibre, but with moss, which can be bought in packets. One of its main advantages is the pleasure to be had from laying it out in the basket: it is the closest most of us will come to knowing what it is like to make a nest. Admittedly, after a short time and despite watering, its mossy greenness disappears and it becomes straggly and lacy – a bit Miss Haversham-ish.

Hanging baskets are filled with the same compost that is used for window boxes and pots. Any of the smaller vegetables will grow quite comfortably in them. Mine have been inhabited by alpine strawberries and a 'herb grove': three rows of bush basil (bushy with tiny leaves) at one end, three rows of sweet basil (larger leaves) at the other, separated by two rows of dill. Earlier in the year huge bouquets of frizzy endive dwarfed the baskets.

Potato watch

Potatoes should be happily chitting away in their eggbox, their shoots growing longer and sturdier. No matter when Easter is, I like to plant them on Good Friday (another form of resurrection), when the Devil is supposed to be busy elsewhere.

Sunshine outings

As soon as the sun comes out, load all the different seed containers and seedlings on to trays and take them outside for a breath of fresh air and a dose of sunshine.

When it becomes cooler and darker, return them to the kindergarten window-ledge shelf.

Parsley check no. 6

By now the seedlings should be ready to transplant into one of the pots, tubs or window boxes. Unless you've become a serious eater of parsley, or a specialist, there is no need to plant them in window-box rows – just here and there between other plants.

There's no need to bother with a trowel when transplanting seedlings into containers. The soil is friable and hands are more malleable than tools – and it is more enjoyable to touch them. Burrow a comfortable-looking hole into the soil, about the size of the parsley container, then put in the seedling,

firming the soil until it looks secure and the stem is straight. Water and leave.

Next morning check to see that the seedling hasn't been blown over, or is keeling over due to thirst or not having been planted deep enough.

First night away

By now the other seedlings will have done a lot of toing and fro-ing on their stretcher-trays between indoors and out. As soon as a warmish evening feels imminent, they can spend their first night out to complete the acclimatisation. At this stage in their life they should be able to stand up to a gentle watering from above with a fine rose watering can.

Runner-bean watch

This is hardly necessary, as beans make such a soundless com-motion when germinating that even the most unobservant seed-sower couldn't fail to notice that something is happening.

The first time I grew beans I couldn't understand why each morning a little compost was scattered on the window ledge beside the container. Had wind blown it there? Or were the cats testing the compost as an alternative to litter? Day by day the compost disturbance increased. What was taking place was more of an upheaval than a germination, as the beans pushed upwards, hardly able to wait to emerge from the compost. (Some seeds are even capable of pushing up asphalt and concrete.)

Final parsley check: reaping what has been sown

Apart from thinning the seedlings during pricking-out, no real tasting has yet taken place. Since then the stems have thickened, lengthened and filled with more sap, while the leaves have broadened and multiplied. To reap what one has sown is a triumphant moment. And the more you pick, the more the parsley will grow.

No matter how much parsley is sown, there is never enough. Sow more.

Seeds to sow now (indoors)

√ Dwarf or French bean (*Phaseolus vulgaris*) – 'Sprite' is good
√ Runner bean (*Phaseolus coccineus*) 'Scarlet Emperor'
√ Cucumber (*Cucumis sativa*) 'Simpson's Sweet Success'
√ Dill (*Anethum graveolens*)

seeds to sow now (outdoors)

- √ American land cress (*Lepidium sativum*) – or save for August sowing
- √ Komatsuna – or save for September sowing
- √ Lettuce (*Lactuca sativa*) 'Black Seeded Simpson'
- √ Rocket (*Eruca sativa*)
- √ Oriental saladini
- √ Vegetable amaranth (dark-grey caviar-like seeds)
- √ Icelandic poppy
- √ Chitting of potatoes (*Solanum tuberosum*)

What to eat now

'Gardener's Delight' first course

This is a combination of small sweet 'Gardeners' Delight' tomatoes, hummus, black olives and a tin of tuna in olive oil.

Making a pond

Plants are so generous in nourishing our senses – sight, taste, touch and smell – that I hadn't realised, until sitting beside a friend's spacious rooftop pond and its fountain, that sound was the only sense missing from my roof garden. It has the reassuring buzz of bees and the deliciously watery sounds made by birds deciding which of the 'orchard' cherries and plums to eat; what is missing is the cool trickling and light splashing of water – especially refreshing when heard in the centre of a city.

I had always looked down on artificial ponds, associating them with eternally fishing gnomes and hollow, fibre-glass rocks. I'd also wrongly assumed that having a pond involved filters, bungs and other underwater equipment. My rooftop friend assured me that this was not so and that a mini-pump fountain is simple to install. It was – in about half an hour.

Before skipping this part of the book, thinking that your balcony is too small, wait. Even the smallest balcony – just deep enough for two feet to stand on – can have a fountain and/or a pond. Window sill owners can even have small fountains or waterfalls. And for those live in flat-chested flats without window ledges and are desperate for the sound of water there are indoor tabletop fountains.

Wall-mounted, puffed-cheeked, dribbling cherubs, lions and goddesses or incontinent little boys do not make particularly attractive waterfalls, though at least the boys make more sense than the others. The simplest and easiest method is to sit the pump inside a good imitation-terracotta plastic tub. It has to be plastic, a) because of the weight and b) because containers without ready-made drainage holes are hard to find. These drainage holes are marked on the plastic and left for the owner to drill or not drill.

My tub is hexagonal in shape, 16 inches (40 cm) in diameter, and 9 inches (23 cm) deep, so there's no danger of drowning. Being plastic, a hole was easily drilled in it, about 1 inch (2.5 cm) from the top, to allow the pump-flex to pass through.

So far all that is needed is a 'mini-cascade' pump, a plastic tub (yours could be smaller than mine) and an RCD (residual current device) to protect against electric shocks – all available from most garden centres.

The fountain has three settings. The lowest and narrowest is 'Intimate Evening', the tallest and widest 'Blackpool Lights' and the third, 'Upturned Jelly'. With an additional piece of plastic hose there could also be a waterfall.

The surface of my tub-pond was going to be covered with chicken wire to support big pebbles and stones, creating a very pseudo-Japanese effect. Then, while looking at the bare face of the water, I wondered about aquatic plants... an aspect of gardening that had always seemed totally alien to earth gardening, and unachievable on a rooftop. However, a few hours later, after reading about ponds, I was walking round an aquatic garden centre – something else that I didn't know existed.

Now, floating on and growing over the edges of the tub is a pygmy water lily, which promises to produce pink flowers (it comes with a guarantee); creeping jenny, which has yellow buttercup-ish flowers; cotton grass – untidy wispy heads, which look bedraggled after rain and badly blow-dried when dry; floating beaver – with, appropriately, beaver-shaped, almost furry-looking, boat-like leaves; and parrot's feather, with a fluffy-dusterish leaf. The above list makes it sound more like a zoo than a pond. If it were larger, frogbit, water crow-foot, turtle head, scarlet monkey flower, toad lily, skunk cabbage and zebra rush could also be added. Apart from the above 'zoological' list, also available are sweet flag, brandy bottle, Joe Rye weed, submerged water soldier, gay feather, fairy moss, yellow floating heart, arrowhead, bugle, water fringe and many more whose names are as intriguing as the plants.

Alternatively, there are plastic water lilies, guaranteed 'to beautify your pond all year round' and no doubt machine-washable – better to be lily-less.

Aquatic plants are divided into five types: 'free-floating', 'marginal', 'oxygenators', 'fixed-floating aquatics' and 'water lilies'. Sounding far more knowledgeable than I am, I can now discuss with other pond owners the merits of free-floaters and marginals versus oxygenators and fixed-floaters, enjoying these five new additions to my vocabulary. I had not imagined that something that is only 16 x 16 x 9 inches (40 x 40 x 23 cm) filled with water, plants and a fountain, could also contain so much pleasure. It is visited several times a day to see what is going on. A lot is (see the June chapter).

The last of the five senses, sound, is satisfied

Good Friday potatoes

The Good Friday potatoes should now be breaking through the surface of the compost, their tips green. As they ascend, add more soil, covering stems but not tips.

The orchard

The 'orchard' will now be in full sail with blossom. It is quite difficult for an uninitiated eye to tell the difference between pear, plum and cherry blossom. Now is the time to find out. Insects are visiting the blossom; the lonely self-fertiliser is making the best of a bad job, preparing to perform the equivalent of an immaculate conception.

Tomato plant roots

If tomato plants were sown in the transparent supermarket trays, by now they will have been transplanted into individual pots. It is then, and while in the transparent trays, that their roots can be observed, growing many times as long as their stems, but only a fraction as thick. This underground root world we know so little about is just as interesting. Over, round and through compost obstacles – lumps and bumps – they go in their search for minerals, salts and water, fragile but determined.

Making more space

Removing the older generation vegetables. Some vegetables, such as frizzy endive become bitter after a time and although they may still look splendid, it is time to remove them. The hanging basket they occupy will be needed for alpine strawberries.

Vegetable bouquets

When removing senior vegetables, don't just put them straight onto the compost heap. Let them spend time in a wide-mouthed bowl as a bouquet. The frizzy endives' bright light-green frilly leaves will fill the bowl and froth over.

Compost: to activate or not

To return to the compost heap and the question of whether to add an activator (something which hurries up the process of decomposition) or not. Some people do, some don't. Organic activators can be bought, though one of the best doesn't need to be. We all possess it: urine. On discovering this, I immediately knew that I was a latent night-soil type and whether the heap needed it or not it received its activator. Mix one part of urine with four parts (some say seven) of water. It must be diluted otherwise it is too strong. Use an old plastic spray bottle to disperse the activator.

First salad feast

The 'Salad Bowl' lettuce leaves should be ready. Remove carefully one by one from the stem. Some people cut the hearts out leaving an inch (few centimetres) of leaves below and wait for new leaves to grow. Rocket should also be ready. Its taste is decisive, even in the smallest leaves.

Usually I don't wash the plants I've grown, preferring to eat them as soon as they're picked, even though they might contain an insect or two. I'd rather eat a couple of insects by mistake than eat lambs' tongues or pigs' trotters on purpose.

Planting plan

This may seem a little grandiose for a few pots and boxes and more applicable to the high-yield, no-taste-no-texture Dutch methods of cultivation. But it is not. One soon forgets what is growing where and will probably end up with too many beans or too few aubergines.

Sketch a little plan of the boxes and pots, jotting down what each contains (i.e. ten 'Sprite' beans in the back row, 'Salad Bowl' lettuce in the front, sweet basil at both ends).

Sowing outside is similar to sowing inside but on a larger scale. Whether it is in pots or boxes, the soil must be friable, its surface even. Some seeds, like night-scented stock, need to be raked into the surface. This can be done with a long-haired cat's wide-toothed grooming comb which resembles a miniature rake. When sowing individual seeds, like beans, which need depth, take a pencil or cane, mark the end with the required depth and make the hole. Some seeds need to be sown in drills (a shallow furrow). Lay a pencil or cane on the surface, push it to and fro to indicate the drill. If the drill needs to be deeper, make the four fingertips walk sideways along the drill while pressing downwards and deepening it, creating little mounds on either side to cover the seeds when sown. Always sow a few more than necessary in case some fail to germinate.

Runner-bean watch

The once neatly patted-down surface of the compost continues to swell and rise, creating fissures and ravines as it erupts. As the beans force their way upwards, pitted boulders roll away, landing on the window ledge. The beans' sturdy stem-necks are still lowered, their solid 'heads' gradually emerging like young heifers'. This is more like a Stanley Spencer resurrection than just eight beans germinating in an ex-Waitrose peach container. It is advisable to arrange one's day around this event rather than relying on the occasional visit.

May – the loveliest of the months

It is always sad when the maternity-ward window-ledge shelf is taken down in May and put away for next year: another spring has gone. There is a lot to be done at this time of year and although the days are longer now, they never seem long enough and by midday half the day has already gone and one longs to elongate what remains.

If it rains, don't stop gardening, just put up a garden umbrella: the drops are usually warm, gentle and spaced wide apart.

second sowings

This is the month to make second sowings. It is tricky to know when to do this to avoid having too much of one vegetable. One method is to sow the second crop as soon as the first has reached the eating stage and you're sure you like it. Some gardeners make repeat sowings every fortnight. I started doing this, jotting the dates down in my diary, 'Sow more 'Salad Bowl' lettuce now' etc., until the diary began to look as though it belonged to a rabbit.

seeds to sow now

When going to a garden centre to buy seeds rather than ordering them by post (owing to insufficient patience), I find it sad to see people wheeling away trolley-loads of already-in-bloom plants, the trolleys three-quarters empty of the enjoyment of sowing.

Seeds to sow now (outdoors)

- √ Abyssinian mustard, also know as Texsel greens (or leave until later for an autumn sowing)
- √ Beetroot (*Beta vulgaris*) 'Detroit 2-Tardel'
- √ Lettuce (*Lactuca sativa*) 'Catalogna'
- √ Mizuna, also known as Japanese greens (again, this could be sown in the autumn)
- √ Mitsuba, also known as Japanese parsley (can also be sown in August)

What to eat now

Chinese sweet-sour radish salad

20 small radishes
½ tsp (2.5 ml) sea salt
1 tsp (5 ml) soy sauce
2 tsp (10 ml) rice vinegar
1 tbsp (15 ml) sesame oil
1 tbsp (15 ml) sesame seeds, toasted, to finish

Top and tail the radishes. If young and tender, cut the green tops into ¼ inch lengths. Using a heavy implement smash the radishes, but not into smithereens; you should still be able to pick them up in one piece. Mix together the all the ingredients except the sesame seeds to make the dressing. Marinate the radishes in the dressing for a couple of hours. Sprinkle with the toasted sesame seeds.

JUNE

Growing saffron

Between June and August the saffron (*Crocus sativus*) corms (underground swollen stem-bases) bought in February can be planted. They like to live in sunny, sheltered places; they dislike shade. You will need 9–10 inch (23–5 cm) deep pots. Fill them with organic compost plus a handful or two of home-made compost, worm casts and a sprinkling of pelletised chicken manure. For those who have pH soil-testers (used to measure the soil's acidity) the pH level should be about seven. The addition of a little lime may help the soil to reach this level, or use ground eggshells (see pages 54-5).

The corms are planted 6 inches (15 cm) deep and 4 inches (10 cm) apart to give them space for reproduction. All the above measurements are just right for containers. Between planting time and September the corms won't object to being on the dry side (remember the other places where they flourish, such as Kashmir and Spain). In September, they will need watering to help the roots grow. In October the first shoots will make their appearance – the right month to have something to look forward to when most other plants are dying down. The soil has to reach a temperature of 41°F (5°C) in order to shock the corms into flowering. This is similar to oyster mushrooms, which also need the shock of coldness to persuade them to fruit, hence their sojourn in the refrigerator (see pages 204-5). What is this need for iciness before fruition?

Flowering should continue for about three weeks. The suppliers of the corms say that it is better to pick the flowers when they are closed, as the saffron will be more intense. In Spain they are picked when open. The drying of the stigma, quite a simple process, is described in a booklet that accompanies the corms – or the La Mancha method could be tried (see pages 135-8).

After flowering ceases, the leaves continue to flourish. From November until April corm reproduction takes place. In May, after all the activity of flowering, producing leaves and reproducing the corms, the leaves die. The plants then need a rest and a retreat. The corms become dormant, their development suspended. Is this similar to the hibernation of animals, when animation is suspended, and to our sleep, which suspends most activity? But when sleep is interspersed with dreams it can hardly be called dormant. Are these three periods related? If so, perhaps more is going on at this time in plants, animals and us than we know.

It is during the dormant period that, every four years, the corms should be lifted, the old ones removed and the new ones sorted, cleaned and dried, ready for replanting.

The first year's flowers are apt to be a bit sparse, but in the second and third year, as the corms increase in number, so should the flowers.

Summary

1 February: order corms.

2 June–August: plant corms.

3 September: water containers to encourage the roots to grow. Look up saffron recipes.

4 October: flowers and leaves appear. Harvesting and drying. First taste. Harvesting may continue into November.

5 November–April: leaves still green, corms reproducing.

6 May: leaves dying down. Corms become dormant, sleeping. Do not disturb.

7 May, four years later: lift corms, clean, sort and dry.

8 June: the story begins again.

Horticultural shepherding

At this time of year everything is gaining momentum, making one realise how short summer is and how important it is to catch it on the wing and take note. This is the month that contains one of the loveliest, yet one of the saddest, days – June 21st, the summer solstice and the longest day, whose next-door neighbour, June 22nd, begins the descent towards the winter solstice and the shortest, darkest day. However, the next-door neighbour of the winter solstice begins the ascent towards spring.

As you are a horticultural shepherd, each day needs to be checked for what is happening and to make certain that all is well. For example, in one 27 x 8 x 8 inch (70 x 20 x 20 cm) window box grows a row of rocket, a row of 'Sprite' beans, a row of perpetual spinach and a row of 'Catalogna' lettuce, which equals thirty-six plants all needing different attention. Tomatoes now require supporting with canes; their in-between shoots (the shoot between the main stem and side shoot) need to be removed to stop them from pushing all their energy into becoming bushes. At the same time cover the tips of all the support canes with silver foil to prevent damaging your eyes (tall *Lilium regale* stems make good supports). When securing stems to support canes, use old-fashioned twine: it is softer and gentler on stems than plastic or metal.

Some small plants may be a bit leggy. Whether the following suggestion is horticulturally correct or incorrect, I don't know. But it works. With a dibber (a hand tool with a pointed end for making holes) *gently* remove a leggy plant from the soil and replant it a little deeper to make it more comfortable. 'Gently' is emphasised because quite a few television gardeners handle plants rather roughly, just plonking them into a hole and shovelling the soil around them as though there's no time to spare. Kittens or Spode china wouldn't be treated this way.

The dibber is one of the most useful of window-box gardening tools. Mine is a variation on the theme, a combination of a generous Stilton spoon and a shoehorn for narrow feet. By placing it into the soil and moving it backwards and forwards, a pocket is created into which a small plant can be slipped.

If dwarf French beans and 'Salad Bowl' lettuce have been sown in the same box, the big butterfly-shaped leaves of the beans and the bosky lettuce may be creating too much shade: trim a few of the lower bean leaves and nibble-prune the largest lettuce leaves to make more light.

Always try to water plants before 'watering' yourself with breakfast coffee or evening drink. Most plants can't turn on taps.

Pond confession

Having a pond opens your eyes to other ponds, one of which (part of a well-known garden) I was passing after having installed mine. And 'passing' is what I should have continued doing. Covering this pond's surface was a thick bright green plant, so dense that at first it appeared to be solid: a flat surface covered with bouclé-knitting lichen. It was so tempting that I was about to step on it. Fortunately my forefinger discovered that beneath the 'knitting' was a pond. As the plant was so dense, I decided that pruning it by a thimbleful wouldn't do any harm. I slipped the 'pruning' into my hand-bag, wondering how it would survive the waterless journey home and the handbag environment.

As soon as I got back, the 'pruning' (called 'Stolen Goods') was immediately placed in the tub-pond, where it made a remark-able recovery... a bit too remarkable, because now, only a few weeks later, the thimbleful is mounting the sides of the pond and threatening to submerge the lily pads. So much for 'Stolen Goods'.

Making logs

This Royal Borough's (free) *Kensington and Chelsea Times* not only converts into plant pots, can be added to compost and used as a wormery 'blanket'; there is another useful job for it, and this is to be recycled into logs for burning on a fire. It is just the right size, 15½ x 12 inches (40 x 30 cm). Any unglossy newspaper may be used – it doesn't have to be royal. As soon as the weather becomes warmer (the 'logs' need to dry in the sun), the log-making can begin.

First you need to buy a Log Maker (see pages 217-19) that will mould the newspaper into a log shape. Most of the work is actually done by the papers, water and sun. All that the human log-maker has to do is to fold about five newspapers horizontally, and place them inside a full-sized seed tray with no drainage holes – or any other similar-shaped container into which they will fit. While pressing them down, fill the tray with water until the newspapers are submerged and have stopped bubbling. After a short time (just a few minutes – though they can be left for longer) they will be saturated.

Remove a folded, soaked paper and, with the fold on the left, roll it up moderately tightly. Take a second folded newspaper and, with the fold on the right, roll this one round the first roll. Putting the folded end first on the left and then on the right produces a sturdier, more even log. Continue doing this until the Swiss-rollish newspapers are the right size to push into the Log Maker. Now follow the instructions for pressing down and squeezing out the water. I stand on the Log Maker for a few seconds until the water has stopped oozing. Remove the 'log' and put it somewhere where it can drain, stay sheltered from rain and dry out in the sun. The logs are ready when they are lightweight. Squirrel them away for the fire-burning months. These building-brick-sized logs, approximately 9 x 4 x 3 inches (23 x 10 x 7.5 cm), take about five minutes to make but will burn for an hour.

Remedies

procrastination

Before doing something unpleasant – for instance income-tax returns or ironing shirts – take a few minutes to examine an individual plant. The eyes will be refreshed, something new will enter the memory and the disliked work will become less onerous. Gardening is also a good remedy for those who are apt to get glued to the past. There is very little time for the past in gardening – it is a present-tense occupation, the future contained within it.

crossness

If you do not feel your usual charming self, repeat the procrastination remedy, but for a bit longer, depending on the degree of crossness, which after a short time disappears. If it doesn't, do some gardening. I've tested this and have been assured by friends and relations that it works... though how the plants feel afterwards is another matter.

tiredness

When feeling tired or listless, do a little gardening, indoor or out: it revives the weary and seems to produce energy. I am in no doubt that there is something healing about working with plants. They restore equilibrium and peacefulness (see note on Horticultural Therapy, pages 210-12). Is there any other activity that, in return for a little time and attention, gives back so much?

Runner-bean watch

The bean 'heads' are slowly rising now, becoming vertical after only eight days. (Although they resemble 'heads', they are the original beans, but much bigger now after having absorbed water.) Anchored by the invisible root inside the soil, the neck-like stems force their way out between the opening bean. The stems are thick, sturdy and sappy, unlike other seedling stems.

After a few more days the seed coats that covered and protected, but which are now too small to fit the swollen 'head', wrinkle and drop off like discarded sunhats. Only a few days ago the 'sunhats' were tough, shiny and resilient.

Two days later: the stem is growing taller and with it, on either side, two plump 'arm' leaves, which are not leaves but larders that will eventually shrivel and drop off. They contain all the nourishment needed for this stage in a bean's life.

From seed packet to saucepan

When the time comes to take a bowl and knife and cut a selection of perpetual spinach, Swiss chard and pak choi, it seems almost unbelievable, when remembering the seeds rattling in their packets just a couple of months ago.

Before harvesting, bring three pots of water to the boil. Never let freshly picked vegetables wait for water to boil. Let the water wait for the vegetables, for it is more accustomed to waiting – in between rocks and in streams. For this first tasting, at least, cook – or rather blanch – each vegetable separately; avoid a muddle of flavours. If chemical pesticides haven't been used there's no need to wash the vegetables, as the boiling water will do that. Don't dilly-dally between picking and cooking (i.e. no telephone calls). And the last 'don't': don't add salt.

Lower the leaves into the gently bubbling water and, as

soon as they turn an even more brilliant green, lift them out with a strainer. This first tasting needs no butter, oil, salt or pepper. It is sufficiently delicious naked, uncontaminated by other distracting flavours. For instance, if salt is added to Swiss chard its slightly sea-ish taste is masked.

The first of the dwarf or French beans should also be ready to eat. Snip them off with scissors or a knife rather than finger-tips, as this causes less damage. There is no need to top, tail or string them. Again, don't add salt and, the last 'don't': don't cover the pan or their loud popping won't be heard. When the popping stops – after about three minutes – scoop out and eat. There is a particular sweetness about just-picked beans.

The natural sweetness in vegetables and fruit (particular-ly that of melons) is always surprising. From where does it come? It is worth remembering that fruit and vegetables also contain the 'taste' of the different weather they have encoun-tered: spring and midsummer sunshine, a variety of rains, frost and slithers of lightning. (There was a distinct taste of hail in a wine I once drank whose grapes had been bombarded by particularly strong storms.)

Seeds to sow now (outdoors)

√ Chicory 'Sugar Loaf'
√ Pak choi 'Canton dwarf' and 'Joi Choi F1' – or sow in August
√ Scarole 'En Cornet de Bordeaux'
√ Plant saffron (*Crocus sativus*) corms

What to eat now

Clotted cream and saffron ice cream

2 egg yolks

1½–2 oz (40–50 g) vanilla sugar (less sweet is preferable, allowing the saffron to have prominence, but use vanilla pods to flavour the sugar)

¼ pint (150 ml) double cream (not too thick, pourable)

¼ pint (150 ml) clotted cream

pinch of salt

small pinch of saffron (about twenty strands, a large pinch will give a bitter taste)

Place the double cream, a vanilla pod and saffron in a saucepan over a moderate heat and bring to boiling point. With a wooden spoon beat together the yolks, sugar and pinch of salt. Pour this mixture into the heated cream and stir until the back of the spoon becomes coated. Do not boil or the mixture will separate. Remove from heat and leave until cold, stirring occasionally to prevent a skin from forming. Remove the vanilla pod. Fold the clotted cream into the custard. Pour this mixture into an ice-cream maker. If not using one, pour into a sturdy polythene container and cover with a lid. When the mixture is partially frozen, stir with a fork until smooth and re-freeze until firm.

JULY

Plants as presents

Don't imagine that when you generously offer friends hand-sown, hand-reared tomato, basil or cucumber plants they will be accepted with open arms. Sometimes they will, but quite often they won't. Friends of the latter variety will politely shy away, saying that they a) have not enough room (they often have twice the size of your own accommodation), b) have not enough time (even though you remind them that they're tomatoes you're offering, not armadillos or some other alarming foreign pet), or c) can't take the responsibility (as though they're being asked to foster a bunch of delinquent children). Lack of green fingers is another reason, despite your suggestion that this might well be remedied by a season of looking after a tomato or two; in fact, they might possibly enjoy the experience. In the end you may have to beg a friend to foster a few plants, guaranteeing step-by-step plant-rearing tuition by telephone, in return for their generosity. Ah well… never mind. Some of the most rewarding recipients of plants are *Big Issue* sellers.

Beijing bean

The other side of the plants-as-presents coin is seen in the case of the Beijing bean. While having a late-autumn Chinese picnic on the outskirts of Beijing, I picked up a few pods and seed heads, having no idea (at this stage in their life) what they were. On returning home, I gave one of the pods to a 'client'-friend at the Battersea Park Horticultural Therapy (now renamed Thrive) centre where I work as a volunteer. Several months later, both pod and picnic forgotten, my friend presented me with a small plant in a small pot. It has furry, ivy-shaped leaves and great potential for growing and twining. A short time after repotting, it produced several blue, miniature, morning-glory-like flowers whose buds are also furry – more like small birds than buds. The flowers are wide awake in the early morning (having succeeded in adjusting to the time difference), then close promptly at about midday – half-day closing for flowers. When they die they leave behind what look like plump, pincushion-shaped fruits, held by five furry, elegantly designed, Ming Dynasty-shaped claws. (How often the number five occurs in the plant world, in the number of petals and the shape of leaves. I'm not numerologically inclined, but have always regarded five as a good number because of our five fingers and toes; the frequent presence of the number five in plants reinforces this choice.)

This Beijing bean, given as a 'seed pod' and then returned as a plant, is the source of great pleasure and interest. In a few weeks it will be taken on an excursion to Kew to be identified. One of its cousins now lives near Bristol. I should very much like to be given seeds from a country to which I'd never been. It makes travelling even more interesting. It might be better to spend time collecting a few seeds than wasting it taking photographs that you and your friends will probably never want to look at.

Feeding the vegetables begins when their flowers turn into fruits – tomatoes, cucumbers and aubergines, for instance – or, in the case of salad vegetables, when they reach the adolescent stage. I used to collect sacks of manure from a city farm, but after a time found too many Mars Bar wrappers included. Apart from the pelletised chicken manure added when filling the containers with soil (see pages 52-3), a little more sustenance can be given now, plus some extract of seaweed (half a capful in 2 gallons or 9 litres of water). As most of this will drain away, another alternative (though both may be employed) is to foliar feed. This requires a small container, called a hose-end feeder (available from garden centres), which is attached to the end of the hose and filled with the seaweed extract. Water and feed are then mixed in the right proportions and sprayed on the leaves. Avoid windy days, strong sunshine and when it is about to rain; also avoid spraying when the beans are starting to flower, for they're too fragile to withstand the weight of the falling droplets. This form of feeding leaves gives a pleasant, seaside-ish sort of smell, intriguing in the centre of a city.

This may be wishful thinking, but there was a definite difference in taste between the seaweed-pelletised manure-fed tomatoes and those fed with a much-advertised chemical feed.

Runner-bean watch

The runner beans have started to bloom in red. Some of the flowers have already begun to turn into beans. Don't wait until they are boomerang-shaped before picking or they will be furry, stringy and tough. Pick when a little bigger than a dwarf or French bean, about 4–5 inches (10–12 cm) long.

Most window boxes, pots and tubs can have a runner bean or two planted inside them. They clamber and scramble up everything even vaguely vertical: wisteria, plum and pear trees, drainpipes, honeysuckle, washing lines and jasmine. As they're quite chameleon-ish, this makes harvesting them a game of hide-and-seek between the leaves.

One of their favourite supports is a *Viburnum* x *burkwoodii* that is now the size of a little tree. A non-gardening friend spotted the beans hanging from the *Viburnum* branches and asked what the plant was. '*Vibeanum* x *burkwoodii*,' I explained to my credulous friend. Also using the *Viburnum* climbing frame is a cucumber.

Bean diary

It is worthwhile jotting down how runner-bean flower buds become edible beans. At the same time write an alpine strawberry diary.

July 6th Tie a piece of soft twine round the bean stem which is to be observed. Green bud is as small as a risotto rice grain; no hint of the flower's redness to come. First alpine strawberry in flower.

July 7th, 8.45 am — Bean bud slightly larger. Red is entering the green, producing a greeny-orange colour.

July 8th — Green tinge disappearing, bean bud plumping out into two fat, little puffed-out cheeks.

Alpine strawberry petals have fallen, leaving a pointed, pitted-thimble, off-white fruit.

July 11th — Bean still swelling.

July 12th — Bean swelling completed. During the night the puffed-out cheeks opened, revealing a snapdragon-ish flower

And so on... — inside.

It would be disgraceful to be asked at the end of one's life how a bean-flower bud becomes a bean and not to know the answer. How many summers has one been witness to this so-called common-or-garden event without ever really having seen it happen?

common or garden

The *Oxford English Dictionary* definition: Used to indicate the most familiar or most frequently occurring kind or species of any thing, which requires no specific name; esp. of plants and animals, in which the epithet tends to become part of the specific name, as in common nightshade, common snake, etc. common salt.

so-called pests

Don't worry about them. People who concentrate on pests fail to see the plants on which they perch. Insects, like so-called weeds, and us must be on this earth for a reason, not just plonked here arbitrarily. There are only two 'pest' anti-dotes I use. The first is an organic insecticidal soap spray with the unpleasant name of Bio Pest Pistol (see pages 217-19), which to date has only been used against blackfly on nasturtiums and against scale on an orange bush. It can also be used against whitefly, greenfly and red spider mite; if used properly, it does not harm ladybirds. The second is a chil-dren's library book on insects. This was consulted when a group of yellow, caviar-sized balls gathered together (like a circular bus queue) on the back of a nasturtium leaf. Thinking they might be another form of black- or greenfly, I was about to aim the only too easy-to-use Pistol at them, but decided to return to the children's library and reborrow the book on insects. The yellow 'caviar' turned out to be butterfly eggs, laid on a nasturtium instead of a cabbage leaf. What happened next took place in August (see page 114-18).

Perfect-lawn mania is another aspect of horticulture with which gardeners are apt to become afflicted, failing to see the lawn for the 'weeds' and molehills. After all, a lawn is only an unnaturally cultivated, comparatively dull crew-cut stretch of Wilton carpet, which is presumably for lying and walking on. If its 'owner' becomes demented by the natural appearance of a few daisies and dandelions and by the grass's constant demand to be mowed, what is the point of it? Where is the pleasure? Trying to force something to behave in a way in which it was never intended to seems a somewhat fruitless exercise. I would not care to be the child of an obsessive lawn owner.

The advantages of sowing seeds in small 8 x 6 inch (20 x 15 cm) trays instead of directly into containers are that it is easier to see what you and the seeds (both before and after germination) are doing, and there is more to observe. The seedlings receive individual attention. The trays can be moved round to follow the sun or find the shade. (This can of course be done at all stages of window-box gardening.)

If you're going away for the weekend and have no one to do the watering, you could take them with you. If they'd be unwelcome, then before leaving get a small plastic bottle, fill it with water, cover the open end with your thumb, turn it upside down and quickly submerge it in the compost.

To plant the trays, follow the seed-sowing instructions on pages 12-13, up to and including stage 5, until the compost has drained. Divide the tray into four lengthways with a pencil, laying it on the compost and pushing it to and fro while pressing down and creating a furrow. Then, depending on the size of the seed, deepen the furrow with the crab-march (i.e. by marching your four fingertips sideways up and down, making little mounds on either side, see pages 75-6). Write the name of seed, the date and, if large enough, the number of seeds sown. Unless the seeds are very small they can be sown individually, or trickled slowly into the furrows. Then with your forefingers return the mounds, covering the seeds.

A 9 inch (22 cm) long furrow full of seeds will be sufficient to stock a 28 x 8 x 8 inch (70 x 20 x 20 cm) window box.

The July 12th/13th seed race:

July 12th	Sowed beetroot 'Detroit 2-Tarde
July 16th, 8 am	Just a hint of a stem
July 16th, 4 pm	Bent over maroon stem showing
July 18th, 10 am	11 up, 2 have leaves. They have started doing exercises, leaves being lowered from vertical to horizontal. Some leaves have a slim maroon outline. Others have maroon backs, but colour soon fades
July 18th, 6 pm	11 were sown, 13 have popped up, ¼ inch (5 mm) tall and already a luminous burgundy
July 22nd	

Orientals versus Occidentals

Sowed 'Sugar loaf' chicory	Sowed Chinese cabbage 'Tah Tsai'
Minute green spots on compost surface	2 leaves visible
18 up, 9 have leaves	13 up, 10 have leaves
15 have leaves which are vertical	12 have leaves
	Third in the race. Its 'true' leaf is more related to the first two, and of similar 'material'

July 13th	Sowed Texsel greens (Abyssinian mustard)	Sowed komatsuna (mustard spinach)
July 16th, 4pm	Nothing visible	Just a hint of something going on
July 17th, 9.15 am		
July 17th, 3 pm	Invisible. However, between 6 pm and 6 am on July 18th, the Abyssinians made their début, unobserved. 9 have come up	
July 18th, 10 am		13 up, 2 leaves appearing
July 18th, 3 pm		18 up, 22 have leaves

Sowed mizuna (Japanese greens)	Sowed 'Salad Bowl' lettuce
First 2 leaves just visible	Nothing visible
	2 coming up, no leaves yet
	12 coming up

25 up, 2 leaves appearing

27 up, 23 have leaves. Did a little thinning. Although mizuna is only ¼ inch (5 mm) tall it already tastes mustardy

July 22nd

Second fastest. It also has sturdy, heart-shaped leaves, but its third true leaf is also faintly deckle-edged; not as pointed as mizuna

July 25th — Third leaf appearing

Winning! It has four leaves and fifth is on its way

The leaves of the Orientals (Chinese cabbage, komatsuna and mizuna) are broad and heart-

Mizuna is in the lead.
First of the 'true'
leaves appeared. It is
quite different from
the first two:
elongated, of a
brighter green deckle-
edged and of different
leaf 'material'.
Questionable
parentage!

Third reddish leaf
appearing

---

shaped. They resemble queues of miniature
stationary butterflies ready to take flight.

July 20th	Sowed 'Black-seeded Simpson' lettuce	Sowed New Zealand spinach	Sowed perpet spinach
		Seed packet says 'Sow in fairly shallow drills.' How deep is 'fairly'?	
July 21st			
July 22nd	The Orientals are revealing signs of their third leaves. The Occidentals are trailing behind		
July 25th			

Sowed rocket	Sowed scarole 'en Cornet de Bordeaux'	Sowed stocks, Virginia and night-scented
	Tried this last year, a bit too bitter. One more try to make certain whether I do or don't like it. Pinked edges	Supposed to be much too late for sowing, but they came up last year at this time
		Starting to germinate

Rocket is the winner
of this league table

salad tasting

Of the different seeds sown, I would sow them all again, except perhaps for chicory, which was a bit bitter for my taste. However, it does have a beautiful way of growing its leaves in a funnel shape (just as sugar used to be wrapped, in a stiff blue paper cone). It would be difficult to chose between the different leaves' sappiness, slightly mustardy and sometimes almost protein taste.

Vegetable flowers

Instead of pulling up vegetables that are about to bolt (run to seed prematurely), let them bolt; then cut them as flowers. The world of vegetable flowers is not really appreciated; they're not given a chance to bloom, so now is the time to let them complete their cycle and examine them properly.

For instance rocket, whose leaves are by now singeing the mouth, has little buff-coloured, propeller flowers: old-fashioned, intricate, strange – as though from the nether world. It is a flower one wouldn't quite trust, unlike an open-faced daisy. Despite this, it will sit happily in a vase for several days. Pak choi has gentle, yellow countryside-scent flowers of which the eaters of stir-fries know nothing. White basil flowers, despite their smallness, smell (not unnaturally) strongly of basil. They're snapdragon-ish in form, having a bouncy platform (or, if seen in profile, what resembles a Habsburg lip) on which small insects can land and stand while feeding.

seeds to sow now (indoors)

See the Orientals versus Occidentals Seed Race on pages 100-107

seeds to sow now (outdoors, or wait until August)

√ Winter purslane

What to eat now

Cold chicken consommé with sour cream and black lumpfish caviar

1 tin of the best chicken consommé you can find,
preferably organic if available
1 carton of sour cream or crème fraîche
1 small jar of black lumpfish caviar
small handful of dill or tarragon

Put the tin of consommé into the refrigerator until almost
solid. Divide between two soup bowls. Top with a generous
helping of sour cream, lumpfish and finely chopped herbs.
Eat the consommé while still in its jelly-ish state. Don't wait
until it has liquefied.

5.45 am visit

The silence that surrounds and emanates from plants is intense: it is not only oxygen and carbon dioxide that plants release.

Whether or not to talk to plants

Not – at least out loud; there's no need to. We do quite enough chattering as it is. As silence is one of the most remarkable of plant qualities (from which we might learn), they probably prefer silent communication. Plants either do or do not sense the feelings of the person tending them. But if bread and mayonnaise are affected by the maker's mood, then it seems likely that plants will be too. As in the case of wheat, yeast, oil and eggs, it is through the hands that 'communication' probably takes place.

A vivid example of silence is present at the Chelsea Flower Show. Apart from the plants' beauty and scent, equally striking are their stillness and silence when surrounded by the uproar of constantly talking and moving *Homo sapiens*.

Pricking out the seed race contestants

market gardens

By now the Orientals and Occidentals will have been thinned out. Another advantage of growing them in small trays is that they can be held up to the light to see which of the seedling silhouettes need thinning. They should soon be ready to prick out. If you are short of space, another method of extending the 'allotment' is to ask a greengrocer for some plastic mushroom-transporting boxes. These are about 15 x 11 x 3½ inches (38 x 28 x 9 cm), are generally green or blue and are not too hideous, even though they're plastic. They already have holes in them to aerate the mushrooms; in fact, there are so many holes that the boxes will need to be lined. Woven imitation hessian sacks (made of polypropylene and the same as those used for lining the château wormery, see pages 152-4 and 217-19) cut to the right size are ideal. Whatever you use, make certain there are sufficient holes to allow the compost to drain.

Fill the greengrocer's trays with compost. If possible water them from below; if not, lightly from above with a watering can rose. Divide them into five rows length- or widthwise and prick out the seedlings with the shoehorn dibber. Any spare seedlings can be planted in other comfortable-looking pots – or eaten.

one of my market gardens contains:

1 row of five komatsuna
1 row of five 'Sugar Loaf' chicory
1 row of five Texsel greens
1 row of five Chinese cabbage 'Tah Tsai'
1 row of five mizuna
Total: twenty-five plants

Beetroot 'Detroit 2-Tardel' needs somewhere a little deeper to grow, so it has been put in a window box. What is going to cause its underground swelling? There is no suggestion of it at the moment; only the bright maroon stems hint at what is to come.

Continuation of the butterfly's yellow eggs story

Most people probably already know this, but, for those who don't, here it is. I'd be happy to be told this drama of metamorphosis as a bedtime story every night.

metamorphosis

The *Oxford English Dictionary* definition: "Pl. metamorphoses. L. metamorphosis, Gr. νεταυδρψωδιs, n. of action. The action or process of changing in form, shape or substance; esp. transformation by magic or witchcraft. Physiology. Change of form in animals and plants, or their parts, during life; esp. in Ent., a change or one of a series of changes which a metabolous insect undergoes, resulting in complete alteration of form and habit."

The butterfly that laid the eggs was probably a cabbage white. After mating for two hours, the male butterfly flies away and the female finds a place to lay her eggs. As central London is not overrun with cabbage patches, a nasturtium leaf was chosen. After laying her eggs, she dies.

egg

The *Oxford English Dictionary* definition: "The (more or less) spheroidal body produced by the female of birds and other animal species and containing the germ of a new individual, enclosed within a shell or firm membrane."

Surrounding the eggs is a substance that sticks them to the leaf. Inside each egg a caterpillar is growing. After about ten days it will hatch via a little hole through which it nibbles its way. It is now a larva.

larva

The *Oxford English Dictionary* definition: "larva. Pl. larvae. [L. larva a ghost, spectre, hobgoblin; also, a mask.] An insect in the grub state, i.e. from the time of its leaving the egg till its transformation into a pupa. In the larva the perfect form, or imago, of the insect is unrecognisable."

"So in his silken sepulchre the worm, Warm'd with new life, unfolds his larva-form." ERASMUS DARWIN, 1731–1802

With sharp jaws, the ravenous baby 'hobgoblin' caterpillar eats the rest of the empty eggshell before starting on the leaf. As it devotes all its time to eating, it grows quickly until it resembles a long, stiff-haired dachshund. Its skin soon becomes too tight and starts to split. It changes skins (to a larger size) four times.

When three weeks have passed it will be fully grown, having reached the halfway stage. It is now a pupa.

pupa

> The *Oxford English Dictionary* definition: " Pl. -æ. [mod. L. A use of L. pupa girl, doll. Cf. Ger., Da. puppe, Sw. puppa, Du. ‹poppe, pop, popje, doll, nymph, chrysalis. An insect in the third and usually quiescent state; a chrysalis."

The 'nymph doll' now stops eating and crawls away to find a safe place. Before settling down, it spins a silk thread that comes from a hole just below the mouth. The silk forms a bed for it to lie on and attaches it to its new resting place.

Now another strange event takes place: the fourth and last skin splits. Inside is a soft chrysalis. After a few hours it hardens, still attached by the silk-thread guy-ropes.

What intriguing, almost secretive words are employed in this whole process.

chrysalis

> The *Oxford English Dictionary* definition: "Pl. *chrysalides* or *chrysalises* but chrysalids is often substituted; cf. orchids. L. chrysallis, chrysalis, Gr. the gold-coloured sheath of butter-flies, deriv. of gold: cf. rush-wick, f. a rush. The state into which the larva of most insects passes before becoming an imago or perfect insect. In this state the insect is inactive and takes no food, and is wrapped in a hard sheath or case."

The chrysalis remains on its silk bed for weeks and some-times months, while inside it a wingless caterpillar begins to change into a winged butterfly. Through the transparent chrysalis case the spots on the future butterfly's wings can sometimes be seen ... that is, if it is going to be a female cab-bage white. Males have no spots.

When the time is ready the butterfly slowly pushes its way out of the case until it splits. When it finally emerges it rests on the empty case, its wings crumpled, damp and slowly unfolding.

After about an hour the wings will have become the right shape, though they are still soft and damp, not ready for flight.

After two more hours have passed, the wings will be dry: the butterfly is ready to fly. The imago is complete.

imago

The *Oxford English Dictionary* definition: "Pl. *imagines* and *imagos*. A modern application of L. *imago* image, representation, natural shape, etc. (First used by Linnæus.) *Entom*. The final and perfect stage or form of an insect after it has undergone all its metamorphoses; the 'perfect insect'."

This extraordinary creature, which is two creatures in one, now has a complete change of food, from spicy-savoury to sweet. No longer will it search for cabbages and nasturtium leaves to nibble, but for nectar to sip, its hollow tongue (which can be extended or retracted) being used as a straw.

nectar

The *Oxford English Dictionary* definition: "Also -er. L. *nectar*, a. Gr. νεκταρ, of obscure origin. Class. Myth. The drink of the gods. Sometimes incorrectly applied to the food of the gods: see ambrosia. The sweet fluid or honey produced by plants, esp. as collected by bees."

"sweet Honey some condens ...
The rest, in cells apart, the liquid Nectar shut."
JOHN DRYDEN (1631–1700), GEORGICS, BOOK IV

Soon the butterfly will mate and the circle will be completed, ready to begin again.

To know this story should make people think twice, if not thrice, before killing a caterpillar. Are not butterflies preferable to cabbages?

Returning to the pond

It is worth having a pond if only to provide a drinking trough for visiting insects, some of which are supposed to be able to smell a pond's existence from 2 miles (3 km) away – does this apply to aerial as well as terrestrial ponds? So far no dragonflies have been alerted to my pond's presence, though wasps and hoverflies (which are ½ inch (10 mm) long and have a similar, but paler, uniform to wasps with one pair of wings instead of two) make up for their absence. Balancing on the pygmy lily pads, these miniature tigers – heads lowered, striped posteriors throbbing – sip. In the early morning the rowing boat-shaped floating beavers are laden with cargoes of dew. A much smaller pond insect (back to the children's library to find its name) skates across the water leaving no footprints on the mysterious surface tension.

In this quite different world of aquatic plants, it is astonishing that buds, leaves and stems can not only survive but develop underwater before flowering above it. Young lily pads spend quite a time sulking beneath the surface. Why don't they rot? Of what sort of 'mackintosh material' are these underwater plants constituted? At least ponds should cause their owners to wonder.

Depending on when the pond was installed and whether or not it has a pygmy water lily, at some time during the growing season, after its pads have ascended to the surface, the lily may need a little nourishment. This comes in the shape of a Café Noir biscuit-sized tablet which, when the pygmy has been hauled up from the 9 inch (23 cm) depths, is slipped into its growing basket. While doing this I also added an oxygenator, called *Crispa elodea*, given to me by a pond friend in exchange for a yoghurt carton of floating beaver. I'd infinitely prefer to be given something from a friend's pond than a bottle of Lambrusco or a box of After Eights. Another advantage: pond presents or swaps are easy to transport.

Potato, alpine strawberry, cucumber, pear, beetroot, plum, artichoke, cherry, nasturtium and tomato report

The 8 inch (20 cm) pots of potatoes will now be filled to within 1 inch (2.5 cm) of their tops and sprouting huge bouquets of stems (called haulms), leaves and perhaps flowers. When they have flowered or begin to show signs of wilting, it is time to see what is going on beneath the soil. First, make certain it is not too dry or too wet, but just right. Second, holding the haulms by the scruff of their necks, close to the soil, gently ease both soil and haulms out of the pot. Embedded in the soil, but just visible, should be new potatoes. Third, disturbing the soil as little as possible, carefully remove one potato, then return everything to the pot, giving it a little shake to fill the potato-less hollow. Now that the potatoes' presence has been confirmed, next time this procedure is repeated, make certain that a pot of water is boiling on the fire before delving inside the pot.

Alpine strawberries (sown early in the year) are still flowering and fruiting in their hanging basket. Wait until they are dark red before picking; their scent is more intense at this stage.

Slicing the cucumber completes the seed-sowing circle, for there, in the sap-oozing slice, are the sculling boat-shaped seeds ready for next season's sowing. There are thirteen of them. Hidden inside the cucumber is a seed mandala – an archetypal design.

The solitary comice pear continues to fatten.

Beetroot, sown on the July 12th. Quite often curiosity wins over prudence and I dig up a beetroot plant (as though transplanting it, giving its stem a wide birth and disturbing the roots as little as possible) just to see what's happening underground. It is then put back as if nothing has taken place. If someone would make transparent window-boxes and pots there would be less need to do this. The result of this prying is the realisation that the beetroots are only just starting to swell – and that their maroon colour stretches right down to their roots, which are a dark pink.

The Victoria plums are becoming heavier, filling with juice. Is sap related to juice? There are thirty-nine plums.

The Waitrose Jerusalem artichoke, planted on April 2nd in a 7 inch (18 cm) tall x 9 inch (23 cm) diameter pot, seems to have mistaken itself for Jack's beanstalk. It is now almost 6 ft (1.78 m) tall and still growing its bristly, pre-shaven stem and leaves, with no imminent intention to flower. Following the potato examination instructions, you may find, tucked secretly inside its soil, some small artichokes. Remove only those that are to be eaten now. As artichokes are nutty and juicy when grated and eaten raw as a salad, ignore the boiling water lecture.

All the cherries have gone, mostly eaten by the birds. Don't worry; it is well worth letting them have their share just to hear them – surely most cities don't suffer from a super-abundance of fruiting cherries. I'd prefer to have more birds and fewer cherries than vice versa.

Eating nasturtium flowers seems vaguely cannibalistic, though if one's prepared to eat the fruits of the flower this is a bit illogical. Flowers used as decoration seem a silly, de trop addition. Vegetables are sufficiently attractive in themselves; they don't need decorating.

However, when the nasturtiums finish flowering they leave behind pods that can be made into alternative capers by preserving them in vinegar – something one might do once but probably not twice, unless capers were suddenly unavailable.

Waiting for tomatoes to ripen can be a mysterious process at times. There they hang on their stems, week after week, plump and green, but with not a hint of changing colour. Days of sunshine beam on them, but the greenness stubbornly persists until, when your back is turned, one day the ripening begins. What is strange about it is that although the tomatoes inhabit different pots and window-boxes they all start ripening at once, as though a tomato-ripening conductor has waved a baton.

Included in this ripening mystery are some American (Amish) 'Brandywine' tomatoes, the seeds of which were given to me by a friend. I couldn't resist sowing them, though with reluctance, when I read that they are considered to be the 'best tasting and some of the biggest tomatoes in the world'. This ungrateful seed recipient did not like their untomato-ish leaves and vast sumo wrestler-sized fruits whose skins bruise, scar and split (i.e. size twenty tomatoes squeezed into size fourteen skins). Being so vast, they take longer to ripen, remaining an unattractive lingerie-pink long after the modest tiny red globes of 'Gardeners' Delight' are being eaten. Fruits and vegetables that are the result of greed-breeding are not sympathetic. Generally they are so heavy that they exhaust their stems, and weigh down and then break the side shoots that try to support them, requiring additional twine and stake-scaffolding. They are the equivalent of cows that have been bred so large that their distorted, painful-looking udders almost sweep the ground.

Plants are generous, producing not only one crop but, in many cases, crop after crop. Why should they be forced into deformity just to satisfy us? Despite my aversion to them, the 'Brandywines' battle on. In this instance there is no need to talk to them. They must sense from the way they are touched that they are not favourites.

There are so many tomatoes now that the tops of the tallest are tied to and supported by a washing line. Six 'Gardeners' Delight' stand in front of a permanently open window, forming a green net curtain.

Seeds to sow now (outdoors)

√ Abyssinian mustard (also called Texsel greens)
√ American or land cress (likes shade so most convenient)
√ Komatsuna (also called mustard spinach)
√ Lamb's lettuce (*Valeriana locusta*, also called corn salad and mâche)
√ Mitsuba (also called Japanese parsley)
√ Mizuna (also called potherb mustard)
√ Pak choi 'Canton Dwarf' and 'Joi Choi F1'
√ Radish (*Raphanus sativus*) 'Red Meat'
√ Spinach (*Spinacia oleracea*) 'New Zealand'
√ Swiss chard (*Beta vulgaris* Cicla Group)
√ Winter purslane (also called miner's lettuce, Indian lettuce and Claytonia)

What to eat now

A small portion of alpine strawberries with Jersey ice cream

4 oz (125 g) alpine strawberries
2 oz (50 g) icing sugar
juice of ¼ lemon (optional)
juice of ¼ orange (optional)
¼ pint (150 ml) double Jersey cream

With a fork, gently crush (not smash) the strawberries. Add
the sugar gradually. It is the taste, texture and scent of the
fruit that should be paramount, not Tate and Lyle. Add
teaspoon by teaspoon the lemon and orange juices, if using;
this emphasises the flavour. Whip the cream until stiff but not
rigid. Fold in the fruit. Freeze.

SEPTEMBER

Compost confession

If the witch-like brew of compost in the plastic sack (see pages 48-50) has become too lumpy and wet, four things can be done to remedy this. One: be less enthusiastic with the urine treatment. Two: mix in scrunched-up balls – not torn strips – of paper; the scrunching provides more air. Envelopes (but not those with plastic windows) and bank statements are the right size. Three: contrary to most compost rules, there's sun-bathing. Open the sack as wide as possible, roll down the edges and, when the sun shines, let the compost bask in it. Four: roll up a *Radio Times*, creating a wick, make a hole in the compost, then place the 'wick' inside to draw out any excess moisture. (The *Radio Times* is also suitable for wormeries, not because worms listen to the radio, but because the wick remedy helps to dry them out if they become too wet.)

Although already-perforated, high-density polythene bags can be bought for the sole purpose of making compost (see pages 48-50), I'm not entirely convinced that they work, except at stage two of composting, which is really the resting and final rotting-down period. For stage one, a small manageable-sized plastic dustbin about 16 inches tall x 15 inches (42 x 39 cm) in diameter with a lid is easier and more effective. Drill ¾ inch (2 cm) holes all round it at about 2 inch (5 cm) intervals, creating an Aertex dustbin. Don't make holes in the top (or rain will get in) and make only a few in the bottom, for drainage. It is much easier to turn a dustbin than a heavy sack – especially if the dustbin has a lid that 'locks'.

More compost ingredient suggestions: wood ash (not coal

ash) provides potassium and lime; old woollen (not synthetic) clothes; the manure and bedding of vegetarian animals (guinea pigs, gerbils and rabbits); ground eggshells (if not being used for a wormery); hair (human and animal) – I only add animal hair (cat combings), human hair being less appealing, but both contain nitrogen. (Some people, particularly spinners and weavers, feel quite friendly towards hair and will collect every available strand. When visiting a weavers' and spinners' annual fair, a weaver pointed to a colleague whose top half was dressed in a dowdy brown, dusty-looking, hand-knitted cardigan. With a mixture of enthusiasm and envy she explained that the cardigan was made of Alsatian combings. Judging by its appearance, the hair had suited the Alsatian better than its owner.)

As more waste is added to the Aertex dustbin, the ingredients become heavier, darker and more unrecognisable.

Nitrogen processes can be difficult to understand, but without it leaves become yellow. Some of a plant's nitrogen comes from the air, which the bacteria in its roots convert into nitrogen compounds. The most interesting converter of nitrogen is lightning, its searing heat forming nitrogen compounds that dissolve in rain and then wash into the soil.

Among the other September crops is the paper log harvest. When the logs have finished drying outside and become lightweight, they are brought inside for a final drying. Mine are laid side by side on the steps of a closed ladder. I haven't been particularly diligent in log-making this year, but there are already thirty-one waiting to be burned, which equals about thirty-one hours of sitting in front of the fire. And there is still time to make more.

Wormery disaster no. 1

There has been quite an upheaval in the wormery. Thinking that they would be better protected from rain in a 'greenhouse' (i.e. a little structure measuring 41 x 20 x 44 inches or 104 x 50 x 112 cm, the sides, back and top of which are enclosed in clear plastic sheeting), I moved them on to its only shelf to share it with the drying-out 'logs'. They were protected from rain, but not from an unusually warm burst of September weather. The result: cremation – and shame.

"I never... trode upon a worme against my will, but I wept for't."

WILLIAM SHAKESPEARE (1564–1616), PERICLES

Wormery disaster no. 2

After being sent a replacement colony of 250 worms by one of the generous suppliers, I moved the wormery back to its original and more clement home beneath the garden table. Thinking that the replacement colony of reds and tigers might like a welcoming treat, I gave them the cats' left-over (but not bad) rather superior tinned food. The 'treat' killed them. Protein poisoning was apparently the culprit. What does it do to cats?

Since then the suppliers of the Can-O-Worms wormery (see pages 217-19) have given me one to test. It is a black plastic, circular, four-storey construction (plus lid) on stilts – something between a high-rise borstal and ultra-modern chalet. Although it is not an object of beauty, it does provide a most interesting way of observing worm life. Starting on the 'ground floor', the worms gradually eat their way up. To do this they have to squeeze through the perforated ceiling-floors. The perforations are only ¼ inch (5 mm) in diameter. At first it was difficult to understand how plump adult worms with ⅓ inch (8 mm) waists were going to squeeze themselves through ¼ inch (5 mm) holes. The suppliers confirmed that the worms would, if there was sufficiently tempting food on the other side of the perforation. And they did: plump worms suddenly elongating themselves into slim, svelte worms.

It was through the Can-O-Worms supplier I discovered the *Worm Digest*, a quarterly American newspaper to which I have not subscribed – yet. It reveals that in North America there are worm symposiums, dinners, galas and tours, videos, conferences (national and international), congresses, CDs (Rot 'n' Roll), consultants (and no doubt counsellors), and worm workshops and networking.

Late September is closing-down and closing-up time: barbecues are scrubbed and brought indoors; deck chairs are stacked; garden umbrellas are made vertical, the imprint of summer caught in the bleached folds of canvas; fans are switched off, dust gathering on the motionless propellers. The arm of the barometer moves towards the left. The air indoors and outdoors is different: there is now a divide. Windows that have been left open all summer are closed, almost. Autumn winds cause the trees to heave and the leaves to make a sea-ish sound. Garden doors swell. Bats hibernate. Plants are fed for the last time, and for the first time bird-feeders are filled with peanuts. Late autumn-sown seeds germinate slowly. If everything else is doing something quite different, what should we be doing?

Not everything is closing down or up at this time. Events that can't be seen are also taking place, hidden inside apparently dead flower heads. Although they may be brown and brittle, these are still alive. Seeds are fattening, their coats hardening in preparation for winter. One of the most beautiful and astonishing is the geranium seed. When the dried, spiky flower heads are ready to spring open, they reveal a still-closed, feather-like wing or sail, at the base of whose mast is a seed anchor. Everything is prepared for flight, landing and germination.

The report

Alpine strawberry plants are looking tired and too relaxed, though they're still producing pointed-thimble triangles of sweetness and scent, but less abundantly.

I am still eating runner and 'Sprite' beans. If the runners become too big and long, just eat the beans and donate the pods to the worms or compost.

Beijing bean flowers are already open at 5.45 am when it is still darkish – more duskish than dawn. The flowers close at 10.30 am. At the base of the plant, the pincushion pods are losing their colour, the sap withdrawing, the pods hardening and browning into fragile, wood-like containers.

The bush and sweet basil are just as prolific as ever.

"Fresh basil... is too precious for so much as one leaf to be allowed to go to waste." ELIZABETH DAVID (1913–92), SUMMER COOKING

There are still plenty of 'Gardeners' Delight' and 'Brandywine' tomatoes on the vines, enough to give to friends who have forgotten the taste of tomatoes. Apologies, of a sort, are due to the 'Brandywine' tomatoes, one of which weighed 12 oz (350 g). When sliced and interleaved with basil and mozzarella, sprinkled with lemon and basil-infused oil, it made a vast breadless sandwich. The soupçon-sized red globes of juice and taste of 'Gardeners' Delight' still remain my first choice.

Two cucumbers are waiting to be picked.

There are plenty of snippings to be made from the Seed Race leaves. Whether one is or is not supposed to pick young beetroot leaves, they are being picked, each a different colour and pattern and particularly juicy. The salad-leaf-nibbling insects and I have come to a unanimous decision: we don't care for 'Sugar Loaf' chicory or scarole; they are too bitter and the only leaves that the insects ignore, so they won't be sown again, despite chicory's beautifully wrapped conical hearts and the squeaky sound its leaves make.

At last the aubergines have started to flower: the sort of wrinkled, pale lilac, yellow-centred flowers that appear in old Germanic tapestries.

The lavender flowers are now faded and dry, their nectar stored in bees' cells in unknown hives, the flowers collected in a bag and scenting the darkness inside a wardrobe, instead of the summer air.

Seeds to sow now (outdoors)

- √ Abyssinian mustard (also called Texsel greens)
- √ Komatsuna (also called mustard spinach)
- √ Lamb's lettuce (*Valeriana locusta*, also called corn salad and mâche) – can be sown until April
- √ Radish (*Raphanus sativus*) 'Red Meat' – can be sown until October
- √ Swiss Chard (*Beta vulgaris* Cicla Group) – can be sown until mid-September

What to eat now

Basil butter

Scented herb butters can be made using most herbs, either on their own or by mixing them. As well as basil, both dill and lemon thyme make good butters.

a handful of basil leaves
unsalted butter
juice of 1 lemon
pinch of salt

Finely chop the basil leaves, not stems, and mix with the unsoftened, unsalted butter, a drop of lemon juice and a pinch of salt.

October gardening

Most Octobers are not particularly tempting months for working outdoors. You have to entice yourself to go out. The sunshine doesn't warm the marrow; it is not for basking in. It is either weak as skimmed milk or brilliant and slanting, painted on but not penetrating, making gardening short and intense.

But there is still quite a lot to be done. Everything vertical – dying tomato plants, beans, cucumbers, basil stalks, the 6 ft (2 m) of Jerusalem artichoke – is made horizontal, snipped into 1 inch (2.5 cm) pieces for the compost to enable it to continue its metamorphoses. The no-longer-green bean stems cling to whatever they have attached themselves to with such strength that they could almost be made into rope ladders – or an alternative to Rapunzel's hair.

Delicate plants, like the orange bush, are brought indoors. So are small pots of parsley and chives.

seed legacies

A friend who always emphasised her lack of green fingers managed, to her great satisfaction, to grow a pot of Italian flat-leaved parsley on her kitchen window sill. As she had too many parsley seeds she gave some to me. A few years later she died. I am still growing those seeds. Of the many seed packets I have, these are special. So is each parsley germination... or reincarnation – more so than the monetary legacy she kindly left me. Seeds and plants could be left in wills for the sake of both the will-writer and the legatee.

Saffron

This, at last, is the month when the harvesting of the *Crocus sativus* stigmas should take place.

> "Thy plants are an orchard of pomegranates, with pleasant fruits; camphire, with spikenard, spikenard and saffron."
> THE SONG OF SOLOMON

One late October I went to a Spanish saffron festival in La Mancha and returned with double the quantity of saffron enthusiasm... plus a flower pot of *Crocus sativus*, still in leaf, which sits contentedly on my London window ledge.

A couple of hours' bus drive from Toledo, in a field beside a road sheltered by grandmotherly olive trees, the rows of crocus grow. From a distance what appears to be a lilac mist hovers low over the ground. Close up, when standing above the flowers, comes the shock of seeing their interiors set alight by orange-red stigma and yellow style. Orange-red, lilac and yellow: one might imagine it would be a gaudy combination. But it is not.

The saffron 'farmers' ('crocers' they used to be called when saffron was grown in England) are plucking the flowers, backs bent double, solid boots placed on either side of the rows of heavy, sandy soil, big wicker baskets filling slowly with the weightless harvest. Behind the pluckers a hill rises. Mounting its side sit the silhouettes of seven windmills, sail-less arms saluting the sky. For the festival, the bare arms will be dressed with sails.

Down a narrow street, behind a door, is a yard. At the side of it beneath a tin roof is a space where a cart or car might be parked. But, instead of cart or car, on the ground is a billowing double bed-sized carpet of thousands of saffron flowers over which intoxicated bees hover. A cloud could have landed. It's impossible not to kneel and bury one's face in the softness of the flowers, inhaling their luxurious, alien but seductive scent.

A few paces away, obscured behind a bead curtain, three people – an elderly man and two women – sit in a small kitchen at a table laid with flowers. They are quietly plucking – not chicken feathers, but flowers: a Spanish still life, by whom? Murillo? The thirty fingers (forefingers and thumbs dyed violet and yellow) appear to work independently of their hands, folding back petals to remove the three stigma. Kneeling beside the table, I try the plucking, copying their movements, my own clumsy and slow-fingered. The older woman corrects me, and with an elegant staccato flick of the wrist – as though demonstrating the playing of a castanet – flicks the stigma decisively on to its pile.

A few feet away from the pluckers, perched on top of an old Calor-gas heater, is a garden-sized wire mesh sieve, inside which the brilliance and juice of the stigmas are being 'toasted' away as the flowers turn into spice. This 'toasting' takes about five minutes, reducing the featherweight stigmas by 80 per cent of their weight. (In 1728 the Saffron Walden 'crocers' took twenty-six hours to do their 'toasting'. The result was called hay saffron. When compressed, it was cake saffron.)

Further down the road, on the other side of another bead curtain, is a small, deserted, bottle-less bar. Behind its empty counter, where bartenders would normally stand, are rows of flower pots of flowering *Crocus sativus*. This is the place from where my pot was bought.

That afternoon the competition to judge the saffron pluckers takes place in another courtyard. Behind iron railings, at a trestle table laid with white cloths, about twelve pluckers sit in white plastic armchairs. The courtyard is full of onlookers, expectation and two big policemen whose holsters contain guns. The pluckers – all women of different ages, though predominantly of the grandmother generation, dressed in their Sunday best – sit on one side of the table. In front of each is a transparent plastic bag puffed out with crocus flowers. The saffron compere, a plump youngish man, rushes to and fro making sure that the contestants are correctly numbered. Tension increases. Finally he shouts, 'Silencio!' The chattering audience becomes quiet.

"Uno, dos, TRES!" The competitors empty their bags onto the table and begin separating. The winner will be the fastest and neatest worker.

The audience presses forward, friends and family encouraging. This is the oddest, most endearing of 'races', between sedate, seated countryside women. Dozens (or rather tens) of agile, hard-working fingers and thumbs move this way and that. The audience's eyes rove up and down the table watching the diminishing piles.

At last the first plucker to finish stands up, flushed, smiling and a little embarrassed. The audience applaud. The policemen smoke.

There will probably be semi-finals and demi-semi-finals before the winner is decided... but before then the last bus back to Toledo arrives. There is something unspoiled about both this competition and the little town in which it is held.

Back in Toledo the crocus is placed on a window ledge in the hotel. Each inhalation of air through the window brings the surprisingly strong, deliciously flowery scent of saffron, reminiscent of this town's Moorish past.

♣

some saffron facts

saffron

The *Oxford English Dictionary* definition: "The ultimate source is Arab. *zakfaran* (adopted unchanged in Turkish, Persian and Hindustani). The origin of Arab. *zakfaran* is unknown; it is not connected with *Çafra'* fem. of *açfar* yellow. The Turkish synonym *Çafran* may however be derived from this adj., and may be the source of some of the European forms."

Crocus sativus, the autumn crocus, is not to be confused with meadow saffron, *Colchicum autumnale*. The cultivated form of

C. sativus, a member of the iris family, is a perennial corm about 1¼–2 inches (3–5 cm) in diameter, planted in mid- to late summer, which grows to about 6 inches (15 cm) tall. A corm is a short, fleshly rhizome, or bulb-like subterraneous stem, of a monocotyledonous plant, producing from its upper surface leaves and buds, and from its lower roots; also called a solid bulb. The plant has six to nine narrow leaves and a long narrow, tubular, blue-violet flower of six petals. The lily-shaped flowers are usually picked when open – though in North Wales they are picked when closed. The wild form, similar to the spring crocus, was used, though it is now seldom found.

Gynaecological details: three stamens are attached to the perianth tube. Stamen are the male or fertilising organs of a flowering plant, consisting of two parts, the anther, which is a double-celled sac containing pollen, and the filament, a slender footstalk supporting the anther. The perianth tube is a structure surrounding, or forming, the outer part of the flower. In the centre of the flower is the pistil, which is a bulbous ovary from which arises a slender yellow stalk called the style. The style is a narrowed prolongation of the ovary, which, when present, supports the stigma at its apex. The style divides into a brilliant orange-red, three-lobed stigma, about 1¼ inches (3 cm) long. The stigma is that part of the pistil in flowering plants which receives pollent in impregnation, either directly on the ovary or at the summit of the style. Propagation is by means of the corms and takes place annually, producing small white, fleshy onion-shaped progeny. Eventually the old corms shrivel and die. The 'crocers' called the stigma (plural: stigmas or stigmata) 'chives'. The

139

Spanish call them clavos (meaning nails; spikes). Are they linked, for the Spanish, to stigmata because of their redness and shape?

"The flowers... opening into five fair broad leaves, with a stile and small threds in the middle of a saffron colour."
SAMUEL GILBERT, FLORISTS VADE-MECUM AND GARDENER'S ALMANACK

Probably first cultivated in Asia Minor, saffron was used by all ancient civilisations of the eastern Mediterranean and by the Egyptians and Romans – in food ("I must haue Saffron to colour the Warden Pies" wrote Shakespeare in *A Winter's Tale*), wine, cordials, liquors, and as a dye, a scent and a drug. In the seventh century it reached China with the Mogul invasion and was used as a drug and perfume. In about 960 the Arabs cultivated it in Spain. In the eleventh century saffron arrived in France and Germany; in the fourteenth century it reached England, brought (it is said) by a pilgrim who had hidden a corm in his hollow staff. Others say that it arrived long before, with the Phoenicians, when tin-trading with the Cornish. In the twenty-first century saffron is grown in Greece, France, Spain, Morocco, Turkey, Iran, Kashmir and North Wales (see pages 217-19). North Wales is hardly synonymous with Kashmir or Morocco, so *Crocus sativus* must possess one of the most equable of temperaments to flourish in such disparate places.

In India saffron is used to treat urinary and digestive problems. It is rich in vitamin B^2 and riboflavin. It is also used as a sudorific (promoting or causing sweating). Joseph Pitton de Tournefort's seventeenth-century *Herbal* warns that an overdose may well cause people to die of laughing. Homeopathic physicians still prescribe saffron for the treatment of uncontrollable laughter ('*Crocus sativus*, three every ten minutes'; however, when there is 'laughing at serious things', take Phosphorous, three every ten minutes). Is this an example of the homeopathic maxim: *similia similibus curantur* ('let like be treated by like').

In fourteenth-century England saffron was considered a commodity of great commercial value. Anyone found adulterating it suffered severe penalties – even death. In Ancient Greece it was a royal colour; Homer and Hippocrates wrote about it. In Ancient Rome it was used as a scent and a dye. When Nero made his entrance, the streets were sprinkled with saffron – no doubt the flowers, not the spice.

"674,4,320 flowers are required to yield one ounce of saffron."
JONATHAN PEREIRA (1804–1853), THE ELEMENTS OF MATRIA MEDICA

More calculations – from different sources:

√ 70,000 flowers produce one pound avoirdupois (450 g) of saffron.
√ 20,000 (dried) stigmas produce 4 oz (100 g) of saffron.
√ 4,300 blossoms produce one ounce (25 g) of dried saffron.
Who does the counting?

Saffron is the most expensive spice in the world. It costs ten times as much as vanilla and fifty times as much as cardamom.

It is astonishing that something so small and fragile, just a whisker-thin filament that has been toasted and shrivelled, should be filled with such powerful colour, scent and taste.

It is convenient for the consumers of saffron that the aching backs and fingers of the saffron farmers do not make their presence known in the taste of a paella, bouillabaisse or risotto Milanese.

What a pack of thieves we are. We steal the stigma from the saffron flower; the eggs from the sturgeon; the truffle from its oak host; the pearl from the oyster; the oyster from its shell and the liver from the goose.

The report

Available to eat and observe now are basil, both 'Bush' and 'Sweet Green'. *Lilium regale* have already made several seed containers: mullion-windowed, airy, yet enclosed. Garlic chives are plentiful, and so are the thin-leaved chives that look less timid. Aubergine flowers continue to ruminate, uncertain whether to bear fruit, though there are signs of swelling. Swiss chard and perpetual spinach are producing fresh leaves. There's also rocket, a sprig of Virginia stock, which must have muddled up the months, American land cress, Abyssinian mustard, a little dill and some flat-leaved parsley. Beijing bean flowers are becoming smaller and paler, a final fling before dying. Winter purslane is producing minute white flowers, in twos, which rest on the heart-shaped leaves. Beetroot leaves are opening (still nothing happening below ground), plus the Jerusalem artichoke – half an artichoke was planted and nine white-fleshed offspring now lie hidden inside the 9 inch (23 cm) pot.

Yields and returns; time is money, self sufficiency, value for money

There's value and value. The above produce, especially at this time of year, is not produced in trugloads but in snippings, clippings and handfuls. The aim of this form of gardening is not to be a threat to the supermarkets; it is not for the sake of self-sufficiency, either, so there's no need to worry about yields and returns.

Even if a £1.25 packet of cucumber seeds produces only four cucumbers, the pleasure in germinating them, watching and looking after them (and all that this entails with propagators and composts) and then finally eating them, is four times four as great, as far as enjoyment and interest are concerned – a high yield, if one *has* to think of yields and returns, which seem to be of paramount importance these days.

Bean in a glass

As seed-sowing possibilities decrease at this time of year, now is a good time to observe once again the miracle of bean germination – even though it is well past bean-sowing time.

But there is another method, in a glass, where the whole process can be seen in even more detail – and close up through a magnifying glass.

Take a clear, straight-sided glass or glass jar (small Kilner jars are good) and line the inside with blotting paper, as though lining a skirt. Fill with 1 inch (2.5 cm) of water. Between glass and blotting paper (which will now be dampened by the water) slip in a runner bean, scar side up. Don't let it touch the water; the blotting paper should hold it in position. Place it on the proverbial warm, sunny window sill. Wait and watch, adding a little water each day.

Don't pooh-pooh this experiment as just something to keep bored children busy. Everyone should observe it, at least once in a lifetime. Here is my bean diary.

October 6th, 10 am — Use either a bought 'Scarlet Emperor' runner bean or one of the offspring of those sown in April. They will be found inside the now-brittle, cinnamon-coloured pods, which are lined with an almost silky protective 'material' – the potential for spring contained within these dry, rattling pods. If ever you need to know how to wrap and pack, look at buds and seeds – they are most ingenious and beautiful, even better than the Swiss and Japanese wrappers. Why is the offspring bean nearly three times the size

**October 6th,
10 am
contd**

of its diminutive parent? The parent is approximately ½ inch (1.2 cm) wide; the offspring 1 inch (2.5 cm) wide. Will it, as the months proceed, gradually diminish in size and intensify its energies? The colour, too, is different, the parent bean's coat being a coffee colour with black speckling, the offspring's a dark pinky-lavender with black abstract doodlings; both resemble Bakelite to the touch.

**October 7th,
3.15 pm.**

Seed coat (also called the case or testa) is starting to wrinkle.

October 8th

Bean has increased in size.

**October 11th,
3.30 pm**

Still no sign of germination. However, between 3.30 pm on October 11th and 10 am on October 12th germination began, unobserved. A white, horn-like protuberance appeared at the side of the scar. This is the root, called the radicle. It points towards the base of the jar. If the bean was turned upside down, it would gradually somersault over itself until it was again facing the base of the jar. This is because it is responding to, and being pulled by, gravity (not because it is seeking darkness).

October 13th,
9 am

Root has doubled in length.

October 14th,
9 am

Root has trebled in length and is pushing the blotting paper away from the glass.

October 15th,
6 am

Root still lengthening; also thickening. Small nodules are developing on the root's upper, thicker part closest to the scar. These are the first hints of root hairs, whose job it is to absorb water and minerals from the soil.

October 16th,
7 am

Nodules have become more pointed; bean continues to drink and swell.

October 17th,
8 am

Bean is nearly twice the size it was when put into the jar. Nodules are lengthening and becoming more root-like. Main root is developing a pointed tip. Seed coat showing signs of becoming too small for what is taking place inside it. The slit from where the root emerged is increasing in length.

October 18th,
8.45 am

Root is now twice the length of the bean. There is nothing fragile or wispy about these root hairs; they look just as determined as the rest of it. Where the

October 18th, 8.45 am contd	seed coat continues to split, something new and green is trying to emerge. This is the shoot, called the plumule.
October 19th, 8.30 am	Bean is 4½ inches (11 cm) long; root is now 3½ inches (9 cm) long. Splitting of the seed coat continues. The 'something new and green' is also dividing. Longest of the root hairs is now ½ inch (1.2 cm) long.
October 20th, 7.45 am	From between the 'something-new-and-green divide', a hoop-shaped stem has emerged, half the size of a little fingernail.
October 20th, 4.15 pm	Hoop-shaped stem is forcing itself out from between the 'green divide'. Easy to see that it is an extension of the root. Hoop-stem is of a browner green.
October 21st, 8.30 am	During the night more splitting of the seed coat took place; it looks ready to burst. But more dramatic than this is the emergence, through the 'green divide', of the 'loop' stem, which has started to straighten and at the tip of which are the wrapped-up leaves, still partially buried within the bean. About ¼ inch (5 mm) of leaf is showing.

147

October 21st, 6 pm
More leaf has pushed its way out.

October 22nd
At some time during the past fourteen hours, the stem has straightened; it is now 1½ inches (4 cm) long and the two still closed-together true leaves have squeezed their way out. This whole process is more like a hatching of some determined bird than a germination. Beak-like leaves still flat and two-dimensional but, when held against the light, the veins needed for its life as an adult leaf are visible.

October 22nd, 12 noon
Tops of the tips of the leaves ½ inch (1.2 cm) apart.

October 23rd, 7.30 am
Stem is upright, 2 inches (5 cm) tall and peering over the top of the Kilner jar. Distance between leaftop tips ½ inch (1.2 cm). True leaves are no longer 'sealed' together but slightly apart, the veins more pronounced. Seed coat's sheen has disappeared; it is an old, much-too-small coat about to be discarded. Inside it the bean continues to drink water, grow and swell. It is almost 1½ inches (4 cm) long.

**October 24th,
8 am**

Stem to tip of leaf is 3½ inches (9 cm) tall. Distance between leaf-top tips is 1 inch (2.5 cm).

**October 25th,
7.50 am**

The two inseparable true leaves have started to part. Between them is the first sign of the growing tip, the 'terminal bud'. Seed coat is torn in several places.

**October 26th,
7.45. am**

Stem to tip of leaf is 4¼ inches (11 cm) tall. True leaves are moving apart; veining is more pronounced, like cabbage-leaf china.

**October 27th,
7.30. am**

Tips of two leaves are 2¼ inches (5.5 cm) apart. Stem to leaf tip is 5 inches (13 cm) long. Leaves are opening. I am going away and won't be back until November 2nd for the next inspection. What will have happened during this time?

**November 2nd,
7 am**

A lot. Leaves are now 3 inches (7.5 cm) long and 2½ inches (6 cm) wide. Stem is 11¾ inches (30 cm) tall and from the tip another three-leaved stem has sprouted. Roots are multiplying, lengthening, fanning out in an octopus manner. Seed

**November 2nd,
7 am. contd**

coat is now more of a casual wrap.
Bean is plump and a healthy bright
green. Tip of shoot is exploring the air,
window frame, light. Perhaps the bean
prefers the caretaker's absence to her
presence and being constantly spied
upon.

**November 4th,
7.30 am**

Kilner-jar method of germination is
excellent, because the caretaker has
both above- and below-ground activities
to watch. Now eight leaves. Stem is 21½
inches (55 cm) tall and fully launched.
Daily watch will concentrate on original
bean and root area. Feel like offering to
help the bean out of its coat, which is
now dry and crackly. But inside it the
'larder' leaves are fat and feeding the
plant. The roots have fanned themselves
around the inside of the jar. The main
root, from which the rootlets sprout,
has turned green, too, the same colour
as the bean; it has also thickened.

**November 6th,
7 am**

Waving stem grows this way and that,
antenna-like, searching for something to
cling to: window frame, curtain, lamp –
anything vertical. When it begins

November 6th, 7 am, contd twining around a support, it will do so in a clockwise direction. Runner beans always twine from left to right. This was noted by an (unfortunately nameless sixteenth-century) engraver in a bean woodcut. It was with some surprise that I saw this; though why should I have been stupid enough to think that sixteenth-century eyes would be less observant than twentieth-century eyes? (Are there any anti-clockwise twining plants? What about Beijing bean? It, too, is a clockwise twiner.)

Bean is splitting open, with striated marks on either side. Only the old coat holds it together. Soon it must be properly planted.

November 11th As the bean is growing in an artificial environment and still insists on wearing its torn coat, I helped it to discard it, enabling the 'leaves' to open. They are still held together at the base, like the palms of two hands.

November 12th, 5 pm Seed 'palms' look less youthful; becoming wrinkled and elderly. They have lost weight. This is not surprising

151

November 12th,
5 pm, contd

as these seed leaves, (cotyledons) are the plant's larder for the early stages of its life and by now must be on the bare side.

Stapling down a few minutes of each day to see what is happening during a minute portion of captured time is worth hours spent surfing the Web. Somehow, it also seems to create more time.

Château wormery

The inauguration of a third wormery has taken place. Not everyone can afford to buy a wormery, but everyone should have the possibility of owning one.

This experimental wormery consists of a 20 x 13 x 7 inch (50 x 33 x 18 cm) wooden box. This particular size was chosen because I was given some old wooden wine boxes (Château Haut-Batailley, 1978) of those dimensions and it seemed right for a little balcony – or anywhere else small. How 'right' the change from wine box to wormery will feel to the friend who gave me the box remains to be seen.

Along the top of the long end about seven holes were drilled. Use the biggest bit available – about the size of a little finger. Along the bottom of the long end another set of holes were drilled. The box was then 'lined' with a postman's sack (made of polypropylene). 'Lining' means just laying the sack inside the box so that its base and sides are covered and worm-proof. Sometimes these sacks are left in the street; Post Office sorting offices might not mind selling or giving them away (or see pages 217-19 for suppliers of these and coir bricks). Coir bricks are made of coconut fibre, which (when water is added) expand into a comfortable, peat-like bedding for the worms. Don't dehydrate the coir brick until the worms arrive. Instead of the brick, mature compost or leaf mould can be used. As long as it is moist, loose and not sodden, it will do.

When the château is ready, order the worms (see pages 217-19). When they arrive, place the coir brick in a bucket and add water, following the accompanying instructions. The brick will expand and break up. Sift through it to remove any lumps. When the coir becomes a bran-like mash, place it in a layer on the base of the château, smoothing the surface. Make a small, nest-like indentation in the centre of the box and place the worms inside, then cover with a little coir. Protect the surface with a damp newspaper or cardboard – the latter is preferable because it has more air in it. Place the château on a couple of lengths of wood, to allow for drainage. Then create a water-proof, but not airproof, cover by cutting a piece of plastic and making an open-sided envelope to wrap loosely over the whole box, leaving the ends open. Secure loosely with a large clip. If possible, shelter the château beneath a table or chair – anything to keep out the rain.

Next day make another nest-indentation in the coir and fill it with a handful of saved-up kitchen-waste food. Cover

153

with more coir and the newspaper or cardboard. Don't disturb the worms. Some wormerers divide their wormeries into neat segments of six or eight (or whatever number you choose) and, depending on how big the wormery is, leave the food in a different segment each time. This is quite a good idea for orderly people, as the worms' appetite can then be checked.

Keep a watch on the coir in case it becomes too dry. If it does, water but don't drench it, remembering how the coir felt when it was first put into the box.

If other types of wormeries are being used, now is the time to protect them from the cold with an eiderdown of bubble wrap – tuck this round the wormery, making sure that air can still enter.

Refreshing the window boxes

After spending spring and summer squashed inside the window boxes and pots, the soil can become compacted and heavy. Before sowing in late autumn, turn the window boxes and pots upside down and sift through the soil, removing any roots and lumps and refreshing it for the new occupants. Add a handful of chicken pellets to encourage the seeds on their way.

(I'm not certain that the so-called self-watering window boxes are such a good invention. They have a reservoir at the bottom, which generally remains full, creating self-bog-making window boxes.)

October–November is the time to order seed potatoes for delivery between December and March:

Potato possibilities

√ 'Blue Kerr's Pink': a blue 'sport' of a pink variety.
√ 'Dunluce': early maturing, and good for potato salads. Can also be grown in growbags. Ready in early May.
√ 'Edgecote Purple': an old Gloucestershire potato, also known as 'Port Wine Kidney', 'Black Kidney', 'Gloucester Flukes' and 'Wigger's Toes'. A rich, all-over vinous purple.
√ 'Etoile du Nord': pink maincrop.
√ 'Magnum Bonum': a parent of King Edward; popular with the Victorians.
√ 'Purple Congo'.
√ 'Salad Red': pinkish flesh, chestnut-ish flavour and texture.
√ 'Salad Blue': blue all the way through, even after it has been cooked.
√ 'Sefton Wonder': russet-skinned and therefore slug-resistant.
√ 'Shetland Black': it really is black.

This list is just a sample; there are dozens more varieties. Choose some, or one, from the 'Museum Collection' of old rare and unusual varieties (see pages 217-19).

Some people think that a potato is a potato is a potato. It is not: they are all different in taste, texture, colour, smell and shape, and deserve to be remembered by their different names, not lumped together as 'just potatoes'.

Small suppliers are more interesting and patient (they don't mind answering questions) and are often prepared to send just a few samples. At the height of my potato-growing passion, I had an interesting relationship with the Macleans of Perthshire. Donald Maclean spent years gathering together the largest private collection in the world of potato cultivars (a cultivar is a variety that has arisen in cultivation) – a potato library. He once exhibited 367 varieties at the Royal Horticultural Society Halls in London. It was he who rediscovered many forgotten potatoes, including 'Salad Blue'.

Occasionally I'd send him a potato brought back from somewhere like Iceland or Egypt. In return he'd send me a handful of rare potatoes, packed in an old custard box. These lumpy presents (he and his wife Margaret refused payment) were most enjoyable to receive.

Donald Maclean died in 1988. His wife continued the potato farm until 1995, when she retired and another husband and wife, G.M. and E.A. Innes, took over the collection (see pages 217-19).

Seeds to sow now (outdoors)

(But only for the patient, as they take much longer to germinate at this time of the year. What are they doing deliberating beneath the soil? What tempts them to emerge?)

√ Lamb's lettuce (*Valeriana locusta*, also called corn salad and mâche) 'Dante' and 'Suttons' Large Leaved'
√ Radish (*Raphanus sativus*) 'Red Meat'

As soon as the heating needs to be turned on, the growing of indoor mushrooms can begin (see pages 160-64).

What to eat now

Raw Jerusalem artichoke salad

This is an unusual, nutty salad.

1 tbsp (15 ml) red wine vinegar
5 tbsp (75 ml) groundnut oil
juice of ½ lemon
1 tsp (5 ml) mustard
sea salt and pepper
Jerusalem artichokes

Prepare the lemon vinaigrette by combining the vinegar, oil, lemon juice, mustard, salt and pepper. Peel the artichokes as thinly as possible. Grate, on a fine grater, into the vinaigrette and mix immediately.

From outdoors to indoors

There are seeds that can be sown outdoors now, but as outdoors is no longer tempting – at least for doing slow things like seed-sowing – now is the time to do indoor gardening. Before going indoors, there is still some outdoor work to be completed (see pages 165-6). Snap up every sunny opportunity; the sunlight will be golden but lined with ice.

Growing mushrooms

I used to do this quite successfully in the sitting room. This doesn't mean that carpets and rugs were sprouting champignons and fairy rings: the mushrooms were contained in a plastic bucket.

These buckets have now been replaced by polystyrene boxes measuring about 10 x 13 x 6 inches (26 x 32 by 15 cm). There are two (maybe more) types of champignons that can be grown indoors: organic and inorganic. They can be bought or ordered from some (not all) nurseries and garden centres. The 100 per cent organic Claës' Champignon Mini Kultur comes from Homebase, while the inorganic Mushroom Kit is produced by Harper Products (see pages 217-19).

mushroom

The *Oxford English Dictionary* definition: "a. F. mousseron usually held to be a derivative of mousse moss. In early use, a fungus of any of the larger umbrella-shaped species, to which the names Toadis hat and toadstool were also applied indiscriminately. Now commonly restricted to the common edible mushroom, *Agaricus campestris*, or to this and species that closely resemble it in general appearance. Some apply mushroom to any fungus supposed to be edible, and toadstool to any that is believed to be deleterious. Certain botanical writers have used the word as equivalent to fungus. The mushroom is a proverbial type of rapid growth."

When growing mushrooms you enter a quite different world from that of plants. Plants belong to the Plant Kingdom. Animals are members of the Animal Kingdom. Mushrooms and toadstools have their own quite separate kingdom, the Fungi Kingdom. The words describing fungi are also different: there are universal veils, vulva, spores, fruiting bodies, fairy rings, mycelium, gills, partial veils, hyphae and many more.

Fungi differ from plants in many ways. They don't have flowers, proper roots or leaves, or anything green about them (i.e. no chlorophyll). They don't have seeds; instead they fruit by scattering their spores. Moulds that grow on damp walls, yeast for baking and brewing, and rusts that attack trees and crops are also fungi. Potato blight – one of the culprits in

Ireland's 1840 famine – is also a fungus, as is dry rot. Penicillum, the first antibiotic, grows on bread and overripe fruit. The mushroom (what we eat) is only a small visible part of the whole fungus. It is the fruiting body, the reproductive part. Most of the fungus, the mycelium, is hidden beneath the ground in a Hades-like world, from which it absorbs nourishment from dead or living organic matter.

"Beware of musherons... and al other thinges, whiche wyll sone putrifie."

SIR THOMAS ELYOT (c. 1490–1546), THE CASTEL OF HELTHE

Mushrooms are strange (one's almost tempted to say creatures), seeming to have one foot (or rather mycelium) in the Animal Kingdom. They appear without warning, silent and cool. Plants don't emerge with a great clatter and bang, but there is always a hint of their arrival: the sprouting of green tips; the squeaking of hyacinth leaves unwrapping.

The polystyrene box will usually contain two bags. Inside one will be spawned compost and in the other 'casing', which is a peat (in the case of the inorganic mushrooms) and chalk mixture. All that needs to be done is to cover the spawned compost (which resembles giant, damp All-Bran) with the casing. Follow the somewhat idiosyncratically translated instructions (in the case of the organic mushrooms). Unfortunately, the organic mushrooms are slightly more difficult to grow than the inorganic, being fussy about the different temperatures in which they need to flourish. A thermometer will be needed. I have several, causing my flat to resemble a cottage hospital: in fact there is one thermometer, and sometimes two, per room – the second to keep an eye on the first.

Apart from George Bernard Shaw's Hertfordshire house, I know of no other house that contains so many thermometers and barometers. If we knew why Shaw was so interested in the rise and fall of mercury, I might know why I am. Mercury is a magical substance and a broken thermometer is something to look forward to. When the vertical liquid silver, held captive in the thin glass tube, is released, it turns into untouchable, uncatchable, star-coloured globules, infinitely more tempting to taste and feel on the tongue than silver-cake decoration balls. But it is lethal.

The organic mushrooms like to begin the first five to eight days of their life at a temperature of 68–77°F (20–5°C), conveniently the temperature as inside the boiler or airing cupboard. Then for one day they prefer temperature of about 59°F (15°C). After this they need to spend the rest of their indoor life, which may be a month or six weeks, at a more temperate 59–64°F (15–18°C). Cohabiting with organic mushrooms can be just as tricky as setting up house with the seedling propagator. If you are too hot or too cold, never mind, just turn on a fan or drink lemon with honey – the seedlings and mushrooms come first or they will die. You, probably, won't.

Autumn and early winter are a good time to grow mushrooms. This is when they grow naturally outdoors and the only time that the near-tropical temperatures indoors are bearable.

> "For wine we left our heath, and yellow brooms,
> And cold mushrooms."
>
> JOHN KEATS, ENDYMION

When the mushrooms' container has been prepared, you might well wonder what is going on inside this apparently unpromising-looking polystyrene box, normally filled with objects such as radios and video recorders, but now filled with compost and spore. Apart from the faint woody smell, there is no suggestion of what is taking place. Beneath the soil or peat mixture, white-ish cobweb-like threads will begin to radiate out from the invisible spores, creating a constellation. These, the mycelium, are the equivalent of roots. Myceliums may be finer than hair or (in some species) as thick as boot-laces. When underground, they can stretch for many yards – some say miles. The mushrooms eventually die, but the mycelium continue to live. When two threads from two different spores meet, a swelling begins and a mushroom starts to grow.

Before this can happen, two to three weeks must pass; the compost should be kept moist, but not wet. Test it by squeezing a pinch between finger and thumb; if no water appears, water it. Keep the box away from direct sunlight. There is not a lot to be done in the way of mushroom caretaking: just waiting, watering and watching.

In the meantime smell the compost. It is springy and damp and has a woodland odour – something never encountered indoors. It makes an even more tempting cats' litter than the seed-compost trays.

Work to be done now

Apart from the worms' monthly treat of ground eggshells, an additional bonus can be a thick slice of bread. Dampen it, place in the wormery and wait. After a few days the bread will be growing furry fungi: penicillin. Lift the slice gently; beneath it will be snuggled a little group of worms, using the bread as an edible air-raid shelter.

Leaves need to be removed – especially from the pond. Some gardeners are perpetually sweeping leaves during autumn and winter. Why not wait until the last leaf has fallen and then sweep? As I don't like putting leaves in the rubbish bin to be thrown away, and don't have enough leaves or space to have a leaf-composting bin, they are collected, then soaked to soften them in a bucket of water, before being added to the compost. This may or may not make it easier for the compost to digest them. Time will tell. But at least the softened leaves vary the compost's diet and texture. The soaking water is used as a cold leaf consommé for the plants.

This is garlic-planting month. If you are going to France, buy some garlic: the robust, ruddy Gallic garlic is preferable to the anaemic-looking, neat specimens found in supermarkets. Divide the head into cloves and plant about 6 inches (15 cm) apart, or singly, in not-too-shallow pots – about 8 inches (20 cm) deep at least. Some gardeners place the cloves on top of the soil, just pressing the root end in; others push them into the soil with just the tips showing.

Sometimes it is possible to buy the bantam egg-sized single-clove Chinese garlic. Try planting this, too. It can't wait to start producing roots.

If autumn-winter salads, such as lamb's lettuce and winter purslane, have been sown, they will need protecting by loosely covering them with a layer of fleece (available from garden centres). This is a soft, lightweight bridal-veil material bought in rolls. It is made of polypropylene and protects against frost, insects and birds, although light, air and water can penetrate it.

sowing 'sensitive plant' seeds

Germinating and growing 'sensitive plant' (*Mimosa pudica*) seeds is supposed to be difficult; even the instructions on the packet say so. Growing radishes is supposed to be easy; they are the first seeds given to children to sow. I've never been able to grow radishes properly, at least in window boxes, but have succeeded with 'sensitive plants'... even to the point where they produce their powder-puff-ish pink flowers.

'Sensitive plant' seeds resemble a miniature version of buckwheat. They need warmth to germinate (70–75°F or 21–24°C), so bring out the propagator again. To entice the seeds back to life, soak them for twenty minutes in warm (140°F or 60°C) water. They can be sown from late winter to mid-spring – of which this month is not a part, but never mind. The soaked seeds are laid on the compost and then pressed gently down, not covered. Germination may take from three weeks to a month.

I grow 'sensitive plants' for two reasons. First, because of the extraordinary way in which their feather-like leaves react when touched by a finger: they gather themselves together, almost closing, and then the leaf descends, as though on a hinge attached to the main stem – or as if suffering from sudden depression. (Is this lowering of the leaves the reason why they are also called the 'humble plant'?) When all finger-touching danger has passed, the leaves rise again. However, they do not respond in this emotional manner when touched by breezes or even wind. In the evening the leaf fronds fold themselves together and 'sleep' – in late winter at about 6.45 pm. In the early morning they open. What, I wonder, is the difference between 'sleep' and being sensitive?

The second reason to grow them is as a proselytiser, to show to people who think that plants are uninteresting and without feeling – just additions to décor. 'Sensitive plants' are the antithesis of the unpleasant, but popular, maintenance-free plants. There is no such thing. All plants are alive and those in captivity need to be looked after by their captors. Only plastic plants are maintenance-free and deserve to be so.

Continuation of 'maintenance-free' lecture: MF plants are on a par with the equally inane pursuits of easy reading, easy listening and easy drinking. If you are too feeble to take note of what is being written, played or in a glass, then the sensible thing to do is to avoid all three. Then neither intellect nor palette will be in any danger of being overtaxed.

The report

Contrary to what one might imagine, quite a few things are taking place in bleak November. The doll-sized aubergines: it is time to harvest them. What, I feel like enquiring of them, are these exotic, southern-belle vegetables doing in mid-winter in a hanging basket on a London roof garden? Lamb's lettuce is slowly germinating. It's interesting to observe this wary germination time – quite different from bursting spring and luxurious summer. Perpetual spinach, rightly named, can still be harvested, and so can Swiss chard. There are also the parsley and chive families – flat and curly-leaved, and garlic and fine-leaved respectively. Also young beetroot leaves. A final handful of runner and dwarf or French beans can be picked – not exactly an offering one would have presented to Elizabeth David, but not to be scoffed at. Lemon thyme, with its sturdy stalks and tiny, less vulnerable leaves is still pickable. So is rocket and winter purslane, that almost violet plant.

Acquiring an antery

An antery (or formicary, see pages 217-19 for suppliers) is an ingenious invention. It is the means by which the life of the worker ants – members of one of the most successful of societies – can be observed indoors and at close quarters. The antery's inventor should be awarded a prize. Every child and adult (particularly those suffering from boredom) should have one. It is included in this book because the owners of most flower pots will have encountered an ant or two and now is a good time to observe them.

The antery is 12 x ½ x 8 inches (30 x 1.2 x 20 cm) and consists of two transparent sheets of plastic held together in a frame. Between the sheets is a narrow space, about ¼ inch (5 mm) wide, which is filled with sand mixed with a little compost. This is where the ants live. Attached to the side of the frame, by 16 inches (40 cm) of transparent tubing, is a transparent magnifier box, which acts as a general playroom-cum-dining-room.

Like the wormery, the ant accommodation arrives first by parcel post. It is simple to follow the instructions and prepare the new home. The tenant-ants will arrive a few days later by letter post (unless you decide to collect your own from a garden, park or field). This double-delivery allows time for setting up the antery, for expectation to increase and for another trip to the children's library.

Inside the envelope will be about thirty yellow meadow ants (*Lasius flavus*), one of more than fifty species found in Britain. They will all be worker ants and all female: all worker ants are female. Yellow meadows aren't yellow, but brownish. When they are not living in anteries, they live in parks, fields and gardens. They are also called hill ants because they build their nests in molehill-sized (or sometimes much larger) hillocks. Other species that are suitable for anteries are black ants (*Lasius niger*). They run much faster than the yellows and are difficult to catch, but they're very hard workers and build large tunnels, so they are good antery performers. There are also red ants (*Myrmica*). These are larger than the yellows and blacks and have a harmless sting. Occasionally the supplier 'runs out of ants' and a few days pass until the stock is replenished.

Basic ant facts to contemplate while waiting for the letter-post to arrive

In the beginning: on a warm spring day, young ants – workers, queens and males – come out of their nests and scurry around. Queens are the largest ants, then come the males, followed by the little workers. The young winged queens and young winged males fly off into the sky for their 'nuptial flight'. Normally the queens mate only once in a lifetime with one or more males. After fertilising the queens, the males die and the young queens then search for a place to build their nests (some will contain two or more queens), where they will stay for the rest of their lives – which may be as long as fifteen years. (In laboratory conditions yellow meadow queens have lived for twenty-five years – sometimes longer.).

When the queen has found a suitable home, she breaks off her wings and digs a small underground tunnel. There she begins to lay her first eggs, which are about ⅕₀ inch (0.5 mm) long. Only queens can lay eggs. She lays two sorts of eggs at two different times of the year: fertilised ones, which hatch into females, and unfertilised ones, which hatch into winged males and queens. While she is on her own she looks after the eggs, cleaning them by licking. She feeds on the reserves provided by the no-longer-used wing muscles – and also on an egg or two.

After a few weeks the eggs hatch into larvae. Inside each larva is a soft body, mouth and miniature jaws. The queen mother (who is also mother superior in this convent community) feeds the larvae. The workers bring water to them. Soon the larvae become too big for their skins and moult. New skins grow.

When the larvae are fully grown (at about ⅛–¼ inch or 3–5 mm long) they spin themselves silk cocoons. The cocooned larva then metamorphoses into a pupa before changing into a worker ant. The queen mother helps the worker daughters to break out of their cocoons. When they first emerge they have soft, pale skins. After a short time the paleness darkens, the skin hardens and the daughters begin their lifetime (which may be a season or a year or more) of work.

"The success of the ant-community depends on a semi-repression of the workers."
J. A. THOMSON, SCIENCE OLD AND NEW

The girl ants all have different jobs. Some concentrate on repair work; some defend the nest; others search for food for the whole colony. Ants are omnivorous, but one of their favourite foods is the honeydew made by greenfly and woodlice. When the abdomens of these insects (called ant-cows) are tickled (or 'milked') by the ants' antennae, drops of honeydew are released, which are then drunk. In return for the honeydew drink, the ants protect the insects by driving away their enemies. Sometimes young caterpillars are taken hostage (when they are called ant-guests) and hauled inside the nest, the captors feeding on the secreted caterpillar juices, while the caterpillars feed on the ants' brood: a good example of a symbiotic relationship. There are also ant millers-cum-bakers. They collect seeds, like wheat, which are taken to storage chamber-granaries. The seeds are crushed and mixed with saliva until they form a paste that is called 'ants' bread'.

The youngest of the girls look after the queen mother, feeding her with regurgitated food. Others wash her with saliva. During this time the queen has been laying more and more eggs – probably thousands. New tunnels are dug and old ones tidied. Some of the daughters are nurses; they feed the larvae and young ants and move the eggs, larvae and cocoons to warmer and drier parts of the nest, supervising the nurseries.

"The lyttelle ant or emote helpeth up his felowe."
SIR THOMAS ELYOT (C. 1490–1546), THE CASTEL OF HELTH

The eggs that the queen mother lays in the summer are different from the first clutch. These are the young winged males and queens. The larvae are bigger and are fed on special food by the nursemaids. When they are ready, the nurses help them to emerge from their cocoons by chewing at them.

The cycle has come full circle.

seeds and other things to sow now (indoors)

✓ Garlic (*Allium sativum*) cloves
✓ Lamb's lettuce (*Valeriana locusta*, also called corn salad and mâche)

seeds and other things to sow now (outdoors)

According to Mr Simpson of Simpson's Seeds (see pages 217-19), the following may also be sown now:

✓ Borecole (*Brassica oleracea acephala*, also called kale)
✓ 'Cavolo Nero'
✓ Broad beans (*Vicia faba*) 'Aquadulce Claudia'
✓ Carrot (*Daucus carota sativus*) 'Amsterdam Forcing'
✓ Swiss chard (*Beta vulgaris* Cicla Group)
✓ Chinese mustard 'Green in Snow'
✓ Garlic (*Allium sativum*) 'Moraluz' and 'Sprint'
✓ Lettuce (*Lactuca sativa*) and salad leaves 'Rougette du Midi', 'Black Seeded Simpson' and 'Mesclun No. 2'
✓ Mangetout (*Pisum sativum*) 'Dwarf Sweet Green'
✓ Radish (*Raphanus sativus*) 'China Rose'
✓ Potato (*Solanum tuberosum*) planting suggestions: 'Jersey Royal' ('International Kidney')

something else to do now: root watching

Suspend a hyacinth bulb above water in a glass container (some are made specially for this purpose) to watch the roots 'knitting' until they almost fill the container.

saffron harvest

Harvesting saffron flowers. In Wales this is done in the early morning; in Spain they were plucking at midday. Some growers pick the flowers when they are still closed but just about to open. Others wait until the flowers have opened. There are two ways of harvesting the fiery, three-pronged stigmas: either snip them, with nail scissors, leaving the rest of the flower intact. Or, cut the whole flower and gently pull the stigma downwards towards the base of the stem leaving the rest of the flower to put in a pot. I prefer this method because the flowers have a surprisingly strong honey scent – just two can scent a room. They can also be observed in detail at close quarters.

The stigma are now placed on a piece of absorbent paper that is then folded to exclude all light. Place it somewhere warm, like an airing cupboard. After two to three days, or when the stigmas have dried and feel brittle when touched, they are put into a small airtight glass jar – preferably tinted to keep out the light. At last they are ready to use.

What to eat now

A simple version of Risotto all Milanese,

Omitting the wine, beef marrow and onion. Although saffron, like truffles, is not a shy spice, the simpler and fewer the ingredients it is combined with when cooking, the better the results.

a pinch of saffron (about 10 filaments)
approximately 1¾ pints (1 litre) organic chicken stock
(using a cube if necessary)
1 oz (25 g) butter
12 oz (350 g) rice (in order of preference: carnaroli,
vialone nano, arborio)
1 oz (25 g) Parmesan, freshly grated
1 oz (25 g) butter
more Parmesan and butter for serving at the table

Pound the saffron filaments and steep in an eggcupful of stock. Meanwhile prepare the risotto. Simmer the two pints of chicken stock in a small-ish saucepan. Melt the butter in another heavy but not too large pan. When the butter is melted, add the rice and stir until coated. Add a ladleful of stock to the rice and stir until absorbed. Continue feeding the rice with stock until it can absorb no more and is of a creamy but not sticky consistency. Some rice – depending on the type and when it was harvested – is thirstier than others. When adding the final ladleful of stock, also add the steeped saffron, butter and grated Parmesan. Stir and serve.

Next year's growing possibilities

This is the month when the days start to descend towards the longest night and the shortest day, December 21st. It should be a favoured day because December 22nd, the winter solstice, begins the ascent towards spring. December is an appropriate hibernation period in which to contemplate next year's growing possibilities. A good place to do the contemplating is in front of the fire, burning the recycled *Kensington and Chelsea Times* 'logs', while the headlines waft up the chimney, as ephemeral now as they were in print.

Apart from sowing successful old friends, like 'Gardeners' Delight' tomatoes, 'Salad Bowl' lettuce, perpetual spinach, Swiss chard and rocket, why not branch out and do something different?

The following is a next-year possibility plan: to specialise in sowing different basils and tomatoes – it would be difficult to find better bedfellows. Specialising is rewarding because it enables the gardener really to get to know one herb and all its possibilities, instead of having just a superficial acquaintance. For instance, most people have no idea how many different basils there are. Here is a list from just two catalogues (see pages 217-19):

Basil list

✓ 'Anise' (*Ocimum basilicum*): decorative mulberry-tinted plant with pale pink flowers and anise fragrance.

✓ 'Sweet' or 'Bush' (*Ocimum basilicum*): small leaves, bushy.

✓ 'Greek' or 'Bush' (*Ocimum minimum*): origin – Chile, small leaves, spherical shape.

✓ 'Fino Verde': has a true sweet basil aroma and taste.

✓ 'Mrs Burns' Lemon': grown in New Mexico, lemon-scented.

✓ 'Cinnamon'; from Mexico, with a cinnamon-clove aroma, light green leaves with reddish stems.

✓ Dark Opal' (*Ocimum basilicum purpureum*): strong basil scent but also decorative, with purple leaves and pale pink flowers.

✓ Greek: grown in pots in Greek homes and restaurants. Compact, with tiny leaves and good scent.

✓ 'Green Ruffles': novelty basil, leaves ruffled and fringed.

✓ 'Green Globe' (*Ocimum basilicum*): origin – Italy, refined bush basil.

✓ 'Genovese' (perfume basil): grown in Italy, almost perfumed aroma and flavour.

✓ 'Holy', 'Sacred Kha Prao' or 'Purple Tulsi' (*Ocimum sanctum*): believed to be the sacred basil from Thailand grown around Buddhist temples. Clove-like scent. Used in India for its medicinal properties for sinus problems and fungal skin infections.

✓ 'Horapha Rau Que' (*Ocimum basilicum*): from Thailand. Anise scent and red stems and bracts with pinky-white flowers.

√ Lemon (*Ocimum citriodorum*): Indonesian kemangie. Grey-green leaves and lemon scent. Use for tea.

√ Lettuce-leaved: the largest- (crimped-) leaved of all the basils.

√ Liquorice: used in South-East Asian cooking.

√ Lime (*Ocimum americanum*): similar to lemon basil but with a distinct lime flavour. Dark green, small leaves.

√ Mammoth: big leaves with a strong aroma.

√ Mexican: thick, glossy dark green leaves. Spicy cinnamon-like scent.

√ 'Napolitano': large lettuce leaf with crinkled edges. Rich, mellow flavour. Grown in the Naples region of Italy.

√ New Guinea: purple flowers, purple veins.

√ Peruvian (*Ocimum micranthemum*): used as snuff in Peru.

√ Purple: violet-brown leaves and stalk.

√ 'Purple Ruffles': dark purple leaves that are fringed and quilted. Pinkish-purple flowers. Strong basil scent.

√ 'Red Ruben' (*Ocimum basilicum*): almost pure purple-bronze leaves.

√ 'Spice': dark green, slightly hairy leaves, very aromatic. Long stems of pink flowers, decorative when dried.

√ 'Spicy Globe' (*Ocimum basilicum*, minimum): bush form with dense globular habit. Extra-strong spicy flavour and fragrance.

√ Thai (*Ocimum species*): cross between cinnamon and liquorice Basils.

√ Tree (*Ocimum gratissimum* = most pleasing): also known as East India or clove basil. Fuzzy lime-green leaves. Small, pale yellow flowers. Burning leaves are used to repel mosquitoes. Can reach 8 ft (2.5 m) in height.

Lists of different tomatoes are more readily available, though for containers it's preferable to keep to the pot-grown varieties; the others can become too domineering.

Something else worth concentrating on would be unusual potatoes (see list on page 155), not those available in shops. Also dill – from a smaller family than basil, but, when added to potatoes, a perfect combination. (If only two herbs could be taken to a desert island, I'd pack basil and dill.)

Dill list

√ Dill (*Peucedanum graveolens*): herbal remedy to assist digestion.

√ 'Dukat' (*Anethum graveolens*): selected for leaf production.

√ 'Fernleaf': a unique strain, producing dwarf plants with dark green leaves.

√ 'Herkules': a cultivated variety. Larger than ordinary dill and deliberately bred so that the 'active ingredient' – the flavour-giving content – is significantly higher.

√ Indian (*Anethum sowa*): pungent leaves, slightly more bitter than normal varieties. Used extensively throughout India and the Far East. Seeds used for flatulence.

√ 'Mammoth': for seed production.

√ 'Vierling' (*Anethum graveolens*): extra-strong stems. Bluish-green leaves. Often used as a cut flower.

Second plan for next year: to plant different fruit. Redcurrants grow well in tubs. So do raspberries, particularly the variety called

'Autumn Bliss' (see pages 217-19). Also try a 12 inch (30 cm) tall *Pyrus communis* 'Doyenné du Comice' pear, available from some garden centres.

The ants' arrival

They arrived by letter post in a small Jiffy bag on which an 'Urgent: Live Creatures' label had been stuck. Inside the bag was the duplicate playroom-cum-dining-room (i.e. the small, transparent, circular magnifier box with lid). Inside it was a little compost and thirty yellow meadow ants – all female workers with wasp waists. The box had a jutting-out tube capped with a plug; so has the antery.

A 1 inch (2.5 cm) piece of the transparent plastic tubing is cut, the plugs removed and then the travelling box and antery are joined by the snipped-off tubing. Any squeamishness concerning ants seems to disappear when your concentration is focused on the actual yellow meadows rather than the idea of them.

Now comes an interesting moment: the crossing of the Rubicon from travelling box to antery. Three workers approach the tunnel. They must sense that something has happened. They seem to be having a discussion. The bravest stands on her back legs and enters the tunnel, but then quickly scampers back to the others. A few seconds later the lone explorer sets off again. This time she goes right into the antery. Will she discover the two introductory tunnels? (These are made when setting up the antery by inserting a pipette-like instrument (supplied) into the sand to make a couple of match-stick-sized tunnel entrances to remind the new residents about tunnelling and give them encouragement.) In the box, discussion continues between the twenty-nine less brave workers.

About five minutes later a few more yellow meadows venture forth. How long will it take them to find the 'playroom' and the 16 inch (40 cm) long transparent tube tunnel? Not long. They are already racing along it, travelling by tube. Perhaps there will be a traffic jam. Two workers meet, going in different directions. They slow down and introduce their antennae, then continue in opposite directions. (Each colony has its own scent, and so does each ant, which is how they recognise each other. How many different ant-scents are there?) Sometimes they turn round in the tunnel, a feat which would be the envy of most London taxi drivers.

The yellow meadows arrived at 9 am. By 10.15 am they had all crossed over into the antery, except for two diffident workers. By noon there was only one left in the box. The others had already started tunnelling.

Ants don't need to be fed often: just once a week, which seems very reasonable, but every week. They like juicy food, particularly apples, bananas and baby food, but only pinhead-sized portions. They also like a little protein occasionally in the form of a dead insect such as a fly. I never imagined I'd be going shopping for yellow meadow ants, but as all four of the above items were missing from my larder, I did a) because they had had a traumatic journey and b) because I wanted to see what the ant manual had said they would do – share the food and feed each other. When a worker discovers food, it leaves a scent trail back to the nest so that its colleagues can follow it.

Post-shopping trip report: pinhead-sized portion of banana placed in 'dining-room' box. So far no sharing of food has taken place; instead a little gorging has been going on, with one ant lying sprawled across the banana mountain in an almost Roman emperorish attitude, probably having eaten too much. When the baby food was offered (a rather unpleasant thick custard concoction of organic 'Vegetables with rice and chicken'), one of the ants got stuck in what must have felt like the savoury equivalent of sinking sand. The most successful menu item is apple – but just not any sort of apple: 'Gala', not 'Braeburn' (we have the same taste). First one ant discovers it, then another; a great deal of racing up and down the 'motor-way' tube takes place. Are they informing each other and/or leaving scent trails? After quarter of an hour the speck of 'Gala' apple is covered with banqueting ants. As far as pears are concerned, their preference is for 'Comice' and 'Conference' – yet again, we agree. Don't kill with kindness and offer too large a portion of food. I did this once, and the result: ant drowned in 'Comice' pear juice. Ants can die of 'ant digestion' and if they are given too much food, they spend less time and less energy on tunnelling.

Do ants drink? The ant supplier is not certain.

Dead ants (due to overeating?) are removed from the antery and placed at the far end of the tunnel, perhaps en route to the 'playroom'. As far as I can see, there has only been one death, which could of course have been caused by old age. Another reason for having an antery is that it creates concern for an individual ant, for a life – not that one can pretend to have become acquainted with a particular individual, but squashing one without thought would now be out of the question.

For those who are not permitted to keep animals, ants could be the answer. There is always something to watch, and observing a quite different world gives another perspective to our own. For a short time each day you leave your world and enter theirs. For people who live alone, an antery could also be beneficial: having something else on the premises besides oneself to think about is better than the alternative. The same applies when taking care of germinating seedlings.

After a week or so, the workers were tunnelling in earnest, rushing up and down the tube with grains of sand, one grain at a time, though they are supposed to be able to lift between ten and twenty times their own weight (the equivalent of a man carrying a car). The result of their tunnelling resembles a rock engraving, or a newly discovered script – or perhaps an engraved, curved version of the London Underground. When the tunnels are ready the workers play an ant version of 'follow my leader', traipsing one behind the other, at almost equal distances, as up and down and in and out of the tunnels they go. The discarded sand has all been moved to one of the plastic boxes, which is now full. When emptying the box, remember that each grain of sand – how many hundreds in just a pinch? – has been transported by two ant feet.

> *"The wisdome of Bees, Annts and Spiders."*
> SIR THOMAS BROWNE (1605–82), RELIGIO MEDICI

Ants don't seem to like getting up early; they are much livelier at 6 pm than at 6 am. They don't sleep, say the experts, but rest or pause – sometimes singly, but generally in a little gathering of ten or so, a few millimetres apart from each other. Although an antery is a type of nunnery, it is no place for a recluse.

Edible seed sprouting

Another germination activity for the height of winter is edible seed sprouting – a good introduction to seeds and what happens to them when they encounter water, warmth, light and darkness. There are several ways of sprouting seeds: in a jar, on a tray and in various sprouting apparatuses (see pages 217-19). However, a glass jar large enough for a hand to enter, plus a piece of muslin and an elastic band, works perfectly well.

Seed sprouting is not a new idea. The Indians, Chinese, Aztecs and Navajo have been sprouting for centuries.

Some seed sprouting books (see pages 217-19) contain toxicity information, while others don't. The potentially toxic sprouts (when eaten raw) are French haricot, broad beans, adzuki beans, lentils, alfalfa, fenugreek, clover and buckwheat. Mung and soya beans are among the least toxic. As long as no more than 1¼ lb (550 g) of raw sprouts are eaten per day (which seems enough for a horse) there should be no problem.

Always buy seed, and grain, that is for human consumption or guaranteed untreated. Seed for sowing is often treated with insecticides or fungicides. If possible buy organic seed-sprouting seed or grain (see pages 217-19).

All sorts of seeds, nuts, beans and grains can be sprouted, such as:

√ Adzuki beans
√ Alfalfa seeds (a complete food rich in vitamins A, B, C, E and K, plus minerals and trace elements. (For more nutritional information read the sprouting books mentioned above.)
√ Almonds
√ Bamboo
√ Barley
√ Black-eyed beans
√ Broccoli
√ Buckwheat
√ Burdock
√ Cabbage
√ Chickpeas
√ Chinese cabbage
√ Chrysanthemum greens
√ Clover, red
√ Fenugreek
√ Kale
√ Leek
√ Lentils, green
√ Lima beans
√ Maize
√ Mexican chia
√ Millet
√ Mint
√ Mitsuba
√ Mung beans
√ Mustard
√ Oats
√ Onion
√ Peas, green and yellow
√ Pumpkin seeds
√ Quinoa
√ Radish – a good crunchy, fiery alternative to mustard and cress
√ Rape seed
√ Rice
√ Rye
√ Salad rape
√ Sesame seeds
√ Soya beans
√ Sunflower seeds
√ Turnip seeds
√ Watercress
√ Wheat

And there are more. The nutritional content of seeds, beans, grains and nuts seems to vary, depending on who is describing them. The sellers of bean-sprouting apparatus seem to endow them with more nutrients than those who are not selling them. One seed expert maintains that 'one half cup of almost any sprouted seed provides as much vitamin C as six glasses of orange juice.'

Begin with one of the easiest, mung beans. As most people know what sprouted mung beans look like, they will know roughly what they are aiming for – though will not achieve! This is because Chinese restaurant sprouts (the commercial ones) are grown under pressure. Another reason to start with mung beans is that their taste and texture are agreeable, unlike some of the extra-healthy seeds, such as alfalfa, whose shoots are thin and almost textureless, resembling leftover pieces of cotton in a sewing box. They taste like the smell of damp cardboard, though obviously this is a matter of opinion.

Sample sproutings: mung beans

Day 1, Sunday   Sunday is a good day to start because for most people it is less busy and offers more concentration. Put a generous tablespoon of beans inside a large glass jar – no more, or the jar will end up with the mung-bean equivalent of rush hour and all the sprouts squashed

Day 1, Sunday, contd

together. Fill with water, shake to clean and remove any wild yeasts, then drain in a tea-strainer or sieve. Refill the jar with water. Soak for twenty-four hours.

Day 2

In only twenty-four hours the beans have doubled in size. Cut a piece of muslin so that it fits over the jar's mouth and secure with an elastic band. Drain the water through the muslin, then examine the beans. Their dark olive-green coats have become a lighter green and some are showing signs of splitting at the waist. The rattling maraca noise they made when dried has changed to a more subdued tone. Fill the jar with fresh water and shake, gently, to clean the beans, then drain again. Most seed-sprouting instructions suggest that the jar should be drained at an angle of 45° and left in this position for a few minutes. Why seeds should like being at this angle I don't know, unless it is the best one for removing the last drops of water. Put the jar in a dark place, but not an airing cup-board which is too hot – under the sink is ideal. Or cover it with a brown paper bag – or anything dark to keep out the

Day 2, contd   light. Repeat the washing, draining and covering each day – morning and evening, if possible.

Day 3   The mungs are almost three times the size of the original bean, plumped-out by water; all the rattling has stopped. Some have discarded their green coats altogether to reveal plump, creamy bodies, others have started to sprout a determined little, hooked, rhinoceros-like horn. Indians eat their mung beans as soon as they start to sprout; the Chinese wait until the sprouts are a few inches long.

Day 4   The horn shoots are now ¼ inch (5 mm) long. Most of the green coats have been discarded. The two parts of the seed are clear to see and look as though they might divide.

Day 5   A healthy white sprout, plump creamy body and, even though discarded, a green coat.

Day 6   Shoots are now 1¼ inches (3 cm) long. At the base of the bean two small legs appear to be sprouting.

Day 7   Small, pointed, close-together leaves –
resembling hares' ears – have appeared.
Eat now, or rather nibble when passing,
as this is when the sprouts seem to taste
most delectable and crunchy. Taste them
at their different sprouting stages to find
out which you prefer. Add them to a
bowl of simmering soup stock and then
eat immediately before they start to
cook. Or make them into a salad by
simmering briefly, draining, then adding
sesame oil, sugar, soy sauce and roasted
sesame seeds.

The glass-jar method seems preferable to the trays,
mainly because the sprouts look happier, their shoots are
whiter, bodies creamier, coats greener. There is no need to go
to the trouble of removing the discarded coats; they add more
colour, texture and taste and without the coats the beans can
look anaemic and fledglingish.

A friend of mine who has always longed to do a little gardening, but lives in a top-floor flat whose windows are window
ledge-less, has become a passionate sprouter, her 'garden' now
being under the sink, on the draining board and on a plate.

Before converting the kitchen into a seed-sprouting
laboratory filled with jars, experiment with a few trial soakings
and sproutings of different seeds in little jars, like those in
which herbs are sold, to see which you like most.

Alfalfa – father of all foods

Day 1   Follow mung instructions.

Day 2   Follow mung instructions.

Day 3   Sprouting has started: the jar is filling with ¼ inch (5 mm) long walking sticks with brown seed-head handles.

Day 4   Sprouts are ½ inch (1.2 cm) long – resemble untidy knitting. Wash, rinse, drain and return them to the dark. May be eaten now or when shoots are a little longer.

Day 5   The mass of brown knitting with white specks has now become a tangled mass of white knitting with brown specs. The shoots are 1 inch (2.5 cm) long and sweeter to taste.

Day 6   Sprouts are 1½ inches (4 cm) long.

Day 7   Minute leaves have sprouted. High time they were eaten.

Almonds

Use unskinned, preferably organic almonds.

Day 1   Follow mung instructions.

Day 2   Almonds have plumped out; they don't
sprout, but undergo a metabolic change
similar to that of a sprout. The crunch
and taste are different, more like a fresh
young almond when it is still milky,
moist and sweet. Definitely worth soaking them. Eat now.

Wheat

Day 1   Follow mung instructions.

Day 2   Wheat is slightly plumper and softer;
looks refreshed. Wash and drain, not
forgetting the mysterious 45° angle;
place in the dark.

Day 3   First sign of sprouting. Looks more complicated than mungs' sprouting, as if there
might be more than one sprout. Wheat is
now soft between the teeth and the divide
between the grain more pronounced.

Day 4 Sprouting three tufts – one probably a shoot and the others roots. It is ¼ inch (5 mm) long. Don't wait too long before eating or sprouts will become stringy and 'elderly' in taste.

✿

For the impatient sower and reaper: growing indoor scissor salads

Unhulled buckwheat grain and sunflower seeds can be sprouted, sown in soil, covered with more soil and left to come into leaf, when they are snipped with scissors and eaten as salad. They are supposed to be more nutritious than lettuce. Green buckwheat contains rutin, for the treatment of high blood pressure, and lecithin for regulating cholesterol levels. Sunflower seeds are almost a complete food and, when allowed to grow leaves, have the additional benefit of chlorophyll.

Follow the mung bean instructions. As soon as they start to sprout, fill a half-sized seed tray with about ½ inch (2 cm) of seed compost, making sure it is damp, but not soaking. Cover the compost with the sprouted grains, using a pencil tip to separate them. The seed tray will be packed with sprouting grains with very little space between them. Cover with a thin layer, about ½ inch (1.2 cm) deep, of compost. Mist-spray with water, and then place inside the propagator. The use of a propagator for sprouting is not mentioned in any of the seed sprouting books, but it works.

Next day a few sprout tips will have pushed their way up through the compost. Two days later masses of sprouts will be forcing not only their way up, but the top layer of compost, too, making it look like an eiderdown about to levitate. Three days later the sprouts burst into leaf. Remove from the propagator and turn the tray clockwise so that backwards-facing stems now face the light. Start trial scissor-snipping.

The most spectacular of germinators – more so than buckwheat or even runner beans – is the sunflower seed. It is difficult to imagine that these large, flat seeds in their smart black-and-white-striped coats could cause such an eruption – and so quickly. The compost rises with the rising shoots, in places leaving the seed tray altogether and becoming vertical, 2 inches (5 cm) away from where it was originally laid to cover the seeds. What is it like for a visiting insect? Between earthquake and big-dipper. At first the germination looks more like a hatching of ducklings as the beak-shaped leaves break through the soil – so much so that it would not be too surprising to hear quacking going on inside the propagator.

Growing wheatgrass

Wheatgrass (when made into a juice) is supposed to be good for us. It would take too long to list its benefits; these are described in Dr Anne Wigmore's book (see page 217-19). If it was taken regularly, one would end up embarrassingly healthy. The juice is available in health and juice bars where large trays of wheatgrass, resembling lawn samples, can be seen growing. But unless you find it beneficial and are prepared to invest in a juicer (see pages 217-19) there is not much point in growing it... unless you are diabetic, as diabetes is one of the complaints that wheatgrass is supposed to help; as one of my cats suffers from this, I grow it – though both cats enjoy the portable wheatgrass lawn. I don't possess a juicer, yet, and as I'm not accustomed to chewing grass, doubt whether addiction to it would ever become a problem. Its taste is not unpleasant – the sort of taste that foods that should do us good tend to have.

Follow the washing, soaking, draining, sprouting and sowing instructions. When wheatgrass shoots first appear they are white and hedgehogish. The next day (still inside the propagator) they will be bright green and upright. On the tips of all their shoots dewdrops (or is it a form of sap?) balance.

If a choice had to be made between growing wheatgrass or sunflower seeds (apart from the medicinal reason mentioned above), I'd choose the latter, more untidy sunflower shoots, which grow this way and that, leaning to left and right or momentarily keeling over. They are more appealing and less military in formation than the regimented wheatgrass. Their taste borders on the delicious: sappy stems, bright, light green fleshy leaves; one could be nibbling a very young 'Primo' cabbage. Taste them at different times during their growth.

The appearance of the mushrooms

One day, while mist-spraying the mushroom box – which is not unlike a small, well-kept field – there will be the unmistakable smell of mushrooms. A few dots of whiteness, probably at the edge of the box, will be seen among the darkness of the compost. If looked at through a magnifying glass, the dots are rounded and smooth, like minute meringues. From now on the speed at which they grow, especially when one's back is turned, is astonishing: a cap, closed in the morning, will be open by the afternoon. A mushroom can double in size in one day. If one were sufficiently sensible, a whole day would be reserved to watch this drama.

The day-old mushroom is covered by the mysterious 'universal veil' (a protective membrane that encloses the young mushroom and gradually breaks down as it expands), stem and cap still joined. As the hours pass, the stem grows taller, the cap becomes wider and the 'universal veil' begins to split as the pressure of upward and outward growth increases, finally revealing both cap and stem. The fungus has been released but the cap is still closed, gills hidden beneath the 'partial veil'. Only a few hours later the last of the 'partial veil' will part, revealing the gills. The mushroom is ready to release its spores. The ring on its stem, and sometimes a skin-like fragment on the cap, is the remains of the partial veil.

These miniature mushrooms are softer than a baby's head, but cool to the touch – mysteriously cool; the compost has quite another temperature, and so of course does the box. From where does this coolness come?

If, at this stage, you can resist thinning them out by one or more mushrooms, then you must be over-disciplined and will miss a taste, texture and sound when eating that you may not have had before, certainly when eating a mushroom: creamy, dense, noisy when bitten into and, of course, cool and only faintly imbued with the taste of mushroom. The sight of them is equally tempting, their whiteness being of a rich, almost powdery white. To do the 'thinning', gently twist the stem away from the compost; what remains in the compost is the vulva. Cover the missing mushroom space with a little more compost. Once tasted, it is difficult not to continue thinning whenever passing the box, consuming these savoury sweets with an almost carnivorous appetite. To add heat, liquid or flavouring of any sort would be absurd.

At the beginning, most of the mushrooms grow at the edge of the box – is this their fairy-ring inclination? Then gradually one or two will appear towards the centre. They seem to like companionship, growing close together, so much so that some of them start off as stubby Siamese twins, only separating later on. Their stems are squat and plump, like babies' legs. An insect taking a stroll across the compost might be quite surprised to find itself entering a dense white wood of squat-trunked 'trees'.

As more and more mushrooms push up through the compost, crowding each other, they press against the sides of the box, which gives some of them a straight edge.

Value for money lecture number two: whether you have one or more crops – or 'flushes' – is a matter of luck, and whether the mushrooms are being looked after properly. But at least you have a new word. A 'flush' doesn't only refer to a flight of birds suddenly starting up, the stream from a mill-wheel, a rush of blood to the face, a glow of light, a hand of cards, but also to a sudden abundance of anything. If there is only one flush it is still worth every penny of your small investment to wait for and see a mushroom grow; then to smell, tend and taste it. There is no point in working out how much mushrooms cost in a supermarket in comparison to the home-grown ones because it is impossible to buy a mushroom with this taste, flavour, texture, colour and 'sound'.

Even Elizabeth David frequently mentioned the cost of food. No doubt this was partly because her first books were written just after the war. But why is it that, of all the endless things we buy, food is the one thing we object most to paying for? It seems to be a combination of the puritanical and the parsimonious. Price is not mentioned in the same way when we buy pillows and sandals (though of course they are not bought so frequently), but then most of us don't eat pillows or sandals: they don't become a part of us.

(Spent mushroom compost can be added to pots, window boxes and tubs.)

Desktop wormery

A desktop wormery is ideal, particularly at this time of year, for those who, since establishing their outdoor wormeries, have developed something verging on a passionate interest in worms – and for those who have not. I acquired one for two reasons: 1) because worms can be observed at even closer quarters, and 2) because the desktop's worms are earth worms (*Lumbricus terrestris*), which are quite different from the wormery's reds and tigers a) they are much bigger, b) they eat mostly soil (extracting their food from it) instead of our leftovers and c) they burrow much deeper.

Although our lives are spent walking, stamping, running, stomping and jogging over the earth, we never – or only occasionally – think of what is happening under our feet. Beneath each acre (0.4 hectares) of grassland an estimated three million earthworms are living – that is approximately 620 worms per square yard (740 worms per square metre). Beneath a football pitch there may be as many as five million worms tunnelling and aerating the soil to allow roots to run and rain to enter instead of just draining away; at the same time they are providing oxygen for themselves. A worm can move about twenty-five times its own weight of soil each year. Charles Darwin (1809–82) made another estimation: each year earthworms bring between 8 and 10 tonnes of soil to the surface of each acre (0.4 hectares) of land. (That is about 15 tonnes per football pitch – not Darwin's estimation.) But when do we ever have the chance to observe this activity, especially at close quarters? The answer is a desktop Worm World (see pages 217-19). It is not expensive and makes an interesting present for adults, children and oneself. However, beware: not everyone will be a delighted recipient, or be in the least eager to take even a fleeting glimpse at your latest present to yourself.

Desktops are made of clear plastic and are 12 x 1½ x 7½ inches (30 x 4 x 19 cm) and have a lid. They could equally well be used as sample aquariums for travelling salesmen selling narrow fish. Surrounding the sides is a removable cardboard cover to provide darkness and privacy. *Lumbricus terrestris* need little attention in the way of feeding and 'maintenance'; in fact, they almost fall into that unsympathetic category of 'maintenance-free', so they are much easier to live with than mushrooms. All the worms need is darkness, coolness, an occasional sprinkle of water and a few potato peelings, grass blades and dead leaves.

The desktop is filled to within an inch (a few centimetres) or so of the top with tiger-striped layers of beige and brown sand, vermiculite (provided) and garden soil. It looks rather like one of those dust-gathering sand-sample ornaments bought at seaside towns, which have no meaning when brought home and placed on the mantelpiece. The different-coloured layers make it easy to observe the worms as they glide through them, eventually mixing them up.

Worms can either be bought with the desktop, or imported from a garden. My version included six Olympic-sized worms, perfect specimens in peak physical condition, each about 6 inches (15 cm) long and correspondingly plump in diameter. (In Australia there is a giant earthworm which can grow to 9¾ ft (3 m) in length. In South Africa there is a worm which is the length of three skipping ropes.)

If worms are included, as soon as they arrive, remove them gently from their travelling box and place them on top of the soil. Replace the lid. For a few minutes they will lie there, like large pieces of rug-making wool, heads slightly raised, pondering where to go. Then down they glide into the earth and sand layers, only the tips of their tails visible; then they disappear. It's as though they've been lubricated by some invisible ointment... which in a sense they have been, as the 'saddle' (called the clitellum, situated about one-third of the distance between head and tail) produces a mucus that helps worms to slide through the soil. As they enter it a slight eruption of the surface takes place to make room for them. (By how many yards would the earth's surface sink if all the worms and their burrows and tunnels were removed from it?) Replace the cardboard cover, put the wormery in a coolish spot and leave it in peace.

How can something so soft, vulnerable and without bones – much softer than one's little finger – glide through earth as though it were blancmange? Try pushing youra little finger into soil.

Worms glide through the soil by contracting and then relaxing their longitudinal muscles, which makes them long and thin as they stretch their heads forward, before contracting and pulling in the rear part of their body, which makes them plump and short. They also have tiny hook-like bristles, called setae, which help them to grip the sides of the tunnel and pull them along. *Lumbricus terrestris* can burrow into the earth to a depth of about 6½ ft (2 m) and in very dry weather they will tunnel even deeper, searching for moisture.

When they have had a few day's rest, remove the cardboard privacy wrapper and they may be seen gliding along, like the most modern of underground trains. The results of their tunnelling – the burrows – can also be seen. These are rounded and smooth, about the diameter of a little finger, comfortable for roots to delve into or even for a White Rabbit to scamper along. *Lumbricus terrestris* is a combination of potholer and miner.

After a couple of days a few offerings may be left on the surface. Potato and carrot peelings, dead leaves or blades of grass – not all at once or it will be difficult to see what has been accepted and what not. Allow one potato peeling per worm and the same with blades of grass. My roof garden is grassless, so grass has to be collected from friends' gardens or parks – I never thought I'd be foraging for worms' nocturnal snacks.

When they are in the wild, earthworms leave their burrows and come to the surface at night; they do the same in the desktop wormery when the inspection of offerings takes place. This is also the time when quite a lot of removal work and rearranging goes on. The six evenly laid out potato peelings will probably have been moved to the side of the desktop. Just the tip of one potato peel will be visible above ground, the rest of this trophy having been pulled down into the underworld, where it can begin composting and be eaten in safety. Earthworms have no eyes, ears or noses, so they cannot see, hear or smell. Instead they sense things by the vibrations on the ground, such as rain drops pattering, which causes them to come to the surface, particularly at night. Occasionally they can be observed mating, lying side by side in opposite directions (see pages 61-2 for mating information).

Until I had this desktop, all the things described above had been hidden and unknown to me. Of course there are excellent films on worms, but even though you sit with your face within a few inches of a television, everything is taking place behind a plastic screen. You can't touch a television worm, smell the earth in which it lives or feed it.

My desktop (it is just the right size to fit into a laptop computer's case) has been taken on several outings to friends, without a great deal of success. The first question is, 'Can they get out?!' (Visits to one's vet are the most rewarding.) Desktop wormeries are equally unsuccessful subjects when brought up at dinner parties – if you are hoping to be invited again. (Compost making is another subject to avoid.)

Toilet-roll mushrooms

Another mushroom to grow indoors is *Pleurotus ostreatus*, the oyster mushroom, which is grown on toilet rolls. Two white rolls are placed on separate saucers; their centres are filled with boiling water until they are thoroughly moistened, but not sitting in water. They are then left to cool for quarter of an hour, helping to sterilise the paper. The inner cardboard tubes are then removed and the holes in the middle filled with oyster spore, an odd white, grain-like substance that does not smell of mushrooms and makes the fingers feel silky after touching it. The rolls and saucers are then loosely enclosed in two plastic bags and placed in a dark, warm (71–80°F or 22–27°C) place, such as an airing cupboard. After ten days the centres and tops of the rolls should be growing short, soft white 'fur', rather like that found on the underside of a baby rabbit. The smell of Andrex has been replaced by a faint aroma of mushrooms.

What has happened is that the oyster mycelium has grown through the paper, breaking down the cellulose and using it as a source of energy. The oyster spawn for growing toilet-roll mushrooms (as well as outdoor 'Shiitake', 'Tree Oyster' and 'Lion's Mane' mushrooms) is available from Scotland (see pages 217-19).

After two to four weeks, say the instructions, the rolls should resemble white Stilton cheeses and smell strongly of mushrooms. They do. Now they are moved from their cosy airing-cupboard accommodation and, still in their plastic bags, placed in the refrigerator, at about 39°F (4°C) for two to four days. This drastic change of accommodation should shock them into the fruiting cycle. Is it the equivalent of frost? After a few days they leave the refrigerator and move house yet again, this time to a cool (50–68°F or 10–20°C), light and humid place. Several holes are pierced in the plastic bags at the places where they touch the rolls. At this stage in their life the mushrooms must not dry out. Mist-spray with water every day, moistening the outside of the bags, especially in the pierced hole areas. This will create humidity and encourage fruiting.

Making a spore print

Different mushrooms have different spores, which can be of various shades. The only way to identify some mushrooms is by their spores – like us and our fingerprints.

Thousands of spores can grow on each gill. Thousands and thousands of spores could fit on a pinhead. Only when the spores are fully grown do they fall to the ground.

Before starting this experiment, examine the underside of a mushroom through a magnifying glass. As far as can be seen, it is sporeless, but miraculous, the fragile gills (similar to a whale's) radiating out from the stem, resting one against the other.

Take a sheet of white and a sheet of black paper and a mushroom (home-grown or bought) – the larger, more adult ones produce more dramatic prints. Overlap the papers, sticking them at the back with Sellotape. Cut the stem-end straight across and a little shorter, so that the downward-facing cap rests almost on the paper, half on the white, half on the black. Cover the mushroom with a bowl and leave overnight. Some fungi release their spores quickly, within three hours; others take a whole day or night.

Next morning remove the bowl and lift up the mushroom; beneath it, on the paper, will be its spore print. The markings are so delicate they could have been left by a feather – certainly no engraver would have produced them. The colour? Shades of Burmese cat. The touch of the spores makes even velvet feel rough. All that is needed now is wind or animals: they are the pollinators.

Some mushrooms continue to rain down spores night after night, the prints becoming paler and paler.

something else to do this month

In addition to visiting the children's library for information, join the Heritage Seed Library (see pages 217-19). Reason for joining: 'to help preserve back-garden biodiversity'.

Modern plants are genetically uniform, and that brings with it the risk of epidemics of pests and diseases. Protecting modern uniform varieties from epidemics, and making sure they meet their yield potential, requires the use of potentially harmful chemicals. Planting a diversity of crops, including several varieties, is an insurance policy against disaster and protects the environment. Freedom of choice: why shouldn't we be free to grow the varieties we want, rather than those on a bureaucratic list?

Legislation decrees which varieties may legally be marketed within the European Union. Heritage Seeds are not registered on a national list, so they cannot be offered for sale but may be obtained by joining the HSL. Some of the library seeds were once commercial varieties that seed companies decided they no longer wanted to offer. Then there are the heirloom seeds, passed down from generation to generation. Others are available commercially abroad, but are denied to gardeners in Europe. The Henry Doubleday Research Association feels that these seeds are too valuable to lose, which is why it established the library, to make certain that they survive.

So it is not only some species of animals and birds that are endangered, but vegetables, too.

Why should all the richness and 'generosity' of the vegetable world be narrowed down to those plants that produce the biggest crops? The seed industry has become the greed industry.

Members of the library can choose six varieties of vegetable each year. The word 'library' does not mean that seeds of the seeds have to be returned, though of course they can be. A report on their success, failure or life from seed to seed might be useful for the library.

The seeds' 'biographies' make them even more interesting. The following will be this year's choice for my window boxes and tubs:

√ *Achocha* 'Cyclanthera pedata': one of the lost crops of the Incas. Produces fruits 2½–6 inches (6–15 cm) long, akin to small cucumbers with a hooked end. A cross between a minty cucumber and a green pepper. (The *Achocha* may be a bit big for a tub, but you can always try.)

√ Climbing French beans, 'Cherokee Trail of Tears': the Cherokee nation was forced out of its homeland in the 1830s on a march that became known as the Trail of Tears. They took their most precious possessions with them; this naturally included their seeds, one of which was this bean with smooth, long, pale green pods that have a chameleon-like quality as they mature. The deep rosy blush turns to a warm chocolate and finally purple, with small black seeds that were usually dried for winter use, although the young pods are also tasty.

√ Lettuce (*Lactuca sativa*) 'Loos Tennis Ball': apparently grown in the 1790s in Thomas Jefferson's garden at Monticello.

√ Babbington leek (*Allium babbingtonii*): not a true leek, but more like a garlic and possibly the wild form of elephant garlic, but a different species from both. The green shoots may be cut and eaten like leeks, while the bulbs can be lifted and used in place of garlic.

√ Sorrel (*Rumex* sp. *shchavel*): from Russia; stays green throughout the year.

√ Tomato (*Lycopersicon*) 'Estonian Yellow Mini Cherry': the seed was obtained from 'an elderly Russian lady at the covered market outside Tallinn'. Typical of a wild tomato.

Continuation of the toilet-roll mushroom story

After eight to ten (in my case fifteen) days of mist-spraying the toilet rolls in their plastic bags, the rolls begin to start sprouting small, pale brownish-grey protuberances, similar to the velvety horns on very young deer. After five more days and a little assistance in directing the 'horns' to the holes in the bags – or making additional holes where the horns appear – they start growing through the holes, a light velvety grey in colour. The cap-heads expand on their elegant stem necks, which lean outwards and upwards from the toilet-roll trunks, like oriental cat-coloured orchids.

And their taste? They have the intensity of a dried Chinese mushroom.

When the last of the oysters has been picked, the rolls are stored in daylight for four weeks at room temperature. During this rest period they should not be touched.

After the four weeks have passed, submerge the rolls, still in their bags, in cold water for eight hours. Then pour away any excess water that has not been absorbed and put them into the refrigerator again (see pages 204-5), following the same procedure as before. This should produce two or three more flushes. If the roll does not fruit the first time, check the moisture level, allow the rolls to rest for a week or two and begin again with the refrigerator treatment.

Horticultural therapy

If, after ant watching, seed sprouting, worm feeding and mushroom growing indoors, you feel in need of some real outdoor gardening, there are plenty of opportunities as a volunteer. It is sad that for some the words 'voluntary work' seem to have a rather patronising, Lady Bountiful association. In fact volunteering is an opportunity to recycle one's good fortune.

It can take quite a time to find the right voluntary work. I tried a form of amateur counselling called Listening Ears, which involved sitting in a dungeon-like room with a red alarm button (connected to the police) at my side and, on the table, between client and listener, a large box of Kleenex tissues. Before being allowed into the dungeon, I had spent two months of three hours a week whizzing at break-neck speed through all the possible problems that might crop up: incest, divorce, death, a mixture of sexualities, suicide and, of course, child-abuse. Armed with a teaspoonful of information, I was then let loose on the unsuspecting public. It all seemed not only dangerous but pointless. (Qualified counsellors – waiting in some hangar for disaster to strike and enable them to pounce – seem equally as dubious as amateurs.)

Then I discovered Horticultural Therapy, as it used to be called, now named Thrive (see pages 217-19 for details), a name that could just as well be used for baby food or an amateur stockbroker.

Here (at the Battersea Park Thrive centre) there are no boxes of Kleenex or red emergency buttons. Instead there are rakes, packets of seeds, a kitchen for cooking the garden produce, a greenhouse, a pond, a vegetable garden, an international herb and vegetable bed, and lots more. It is a working, not a display, garden.

The people who come to Thrive are men and women, young and old, of different nationalities, races, religions and backgrounds. They may have physical or mental problems, or both. You may or may not learn what those problems are. When something is given a label – such as schizophrenia – what does it really mean, to an amateur? You will probably sense more about the person and their problem when sweeping leaves, pricking out seeds or making soup together than you could from hours of conversation – or, rather, passive listening – across a table.

Ray had a major stroke and was left almost immobile, with no feeling in his left hand. Boiling water felt cold; sharp knives felt blunt. It was while growing 'sensitive plants' that some of the feeling in his hand returned. He noticed that the slightest touching of the plant's leaves made them descend. He also noticed that he could feel these fragile leaves. It is interesting that it was the lightest of touches he could feel, whereas boiling water or the blade of a sharp knife went unnoticed.

Jack, who used to come once a week and whose confidence was at 'rock bottom', would plant something and then spend the rest of the week at home in sheltered housing worrying about the plant, feeling certain that it had died. It was with surprise that the following week he found it hadn't. But then he'd remind himself that, if it hadn't died last week, it probably would next. The plant continued to live.

Daisy is young and deaf and cannot speak, except with her hands and smile.

Why is it that the majority of people we work with at Thrive are so thoughtful and grateful, despite their problems? Being there is a good antidote to grumbling. I never imagined that I'd be able to work with people suffering from mental and physical disabilities, but quite often it's less complicated than working with people without.

seeds and other things to sow now (indoors)

√ Italian plain-leaved parsley (*Petroselinum crispum*)
√ 'Sensitive plants' (*Mimosa pudica*)
√ Champignons and oyster mushrooms (*Pleurotus ostreatus*)
√ Sprouting seeds, beans, nuts and cereals (see page 187)
√ Lemongrass – find a specimen with a plump, bulbous end;
  place in water until roots develop; plant outside in spring
√ Sweet potatoes (*Ipomoea batatas*) and edoes
√ Root ginger – put in a screwtop jar in the refrigerator and
  wait until roots appear; plant in a pot.

What to eat now

Pinenut soup

4 oz (100 g) pinenuts
1½ pints (850 ml) organic chicken or vegetable stock (cubes will do)
¼ pint (150 ml) organic Jersey double cream

Liquidise the pinenuts with a small amount of the stock to
begin with, gradually adding the rest. Pour the cream into
this mixture and heat, but do not boil. If stock cubes have
been used, salt and pepper will not be needed.

"Nothing satisfies the man who is not satisfied with a little."
EPICURUS (341–271 BC)

Seed-sowing, fungi-growing and seed-sprouting diary

The sowing times given are those printed on the back of the seed packets. Obviously where you live – north, south, beside the sea, in a town – will make a difference and you will have to add or subtract months to those suggested.

Seed	Sowing time/place
√ Italian plain-leaved parsley	√ any time/indoors
√ Seed sprouting and scissor salads	√ any time/indoors
√ Greengrocer/supermarket vegetables – root ginger, lemongrass, sweet potatoes	√ any time/indoors
√ 'Gardeners' Delight' tomatoes	√ January–March/indoors
√ Sweet peas (*Lathyrus odoratus*)	√ January–mid-May/indoors
√ Garlic chives	√ February–April/indoors
√ 'Sweet Green' basil	√ February–April/indoors
√ 'Bush' basil	√ February–April/indoors
√ Alpine strawberries	√ February/indoors
√ 'Sensitive plants' (*Mimosa pudica*)	√ February–April/indoors
√ Busy Lizzie (*Impatiens*)	√ February–April/indoors
√ 'Slim Jim' aubergine	√ March/indoors
√ Red and green 'Salad Bowl' lettuce	√ March–July/outdoors
√ Perpetual spinach	√ March–mid-July/outdoors
√ 'New Zealand' spinach	√ March–August/outdoors

Seed	Sowing time/place
√ 'Jacob's Coat' Swiss chard	√ March–mid-September/ outdoors
√ Baby parsnips	√ March–mid-June/outdoors
√ 'Sweet Scented' mignonette	√ March–May/outdoors
√ Nasturtiums	√ March/indoors; April–May/outdoors
√ Night-scented stock	√ mid-March–May/outdoors
√ Virginia stock	√ mid-March–May/outdoors
√ 'Sprite' dwarf or French bean	√ April/indoors; mid-May/ outdoors
√ 'Scarlet Emperor' runner bean	√ April/indoors; May–June/ outdoors
√ American land cress (Belle Isle, early winter, upland cress)	√ April or August/outdoors
√ 'Simpson's Sweet Success' and 'Petita F1' cucumbers	√ April/indoors
√ Annual dill 'Bouquet'	√ April/indoors; May/outdoors
√ Komatsuna (mustard spinach)	√ April–September/outdoors
√ 'Black Seeded Simpson' lettuce	√ April/outdoors
√ Potatoes	√ April (plant on Good Friday)
√ Rocket (arugula, Italian cress)	√ April–mid-July/outdoors
√ Oriental saladini	√ April–June/outdoors
√ Vegetable amaranth	√ April–June/outdoors
√ 'Iceland Giant' poppy	√ April–early-June/outdoors
√ Baby kohl-rabi	√ April–mid-August/outdoors
√ Abyssinian mustard (Texsel greens)	√ May–September/outdoors

seed	sowing time/place
✓ 'Detroit 2-Tardel' beetroot	✓ May–July/outdoors
✓ 'Catalogna' lettuce	✓ May–June/outdoors
✓ Mizuna (Japanese greens, potherb mustard)	✓ May–August/outdoors; September–April/under glass
✓ Mitsuba (Japanese parsley)	✓ May or August/outdoors
✓ Chicory 'Sugar Loaf'	✓ June–July/outdoors
✓ 'Canton Dwarf', 'Joi Choi F1' pak choi	✓ June–August/outdoors
✓ 'En Cornet de Bordeaux' scarole	✓ June–July/outdoors
✓ Saffron (*Crocus sativus*)	✓ June–August/outdoors
✓ 'Tah Tsai' Chinese cabbage	✓ July/outdoors
✓ Winter purslane (miner's lettuce, Indian lettuce, Claytonia)	✓ July–August/outdoors
✓ Lamb's lettuce (corn salad mâche), large-leaved	✓ mid-August–October/outdoors
✓ Radish 'Red Meat'	✓ August–October/outdoors
✓ 'Dante' corn salad	✓ September–April/outdoors
✓ Champignon and toilet- roll oyster mushrooms	✓ October–April (as soon as the heating is on)/indoors
✓ Potatoes	✓ October (order seed potatoes)
✓ Garlic	✓ November (plant cloves)
✓ Order seeds	✓ December

stockists and suppliers

Chase Organics

Riverdene Business Park
Molesey Road
Hersham, Surrey KT12 4RG
Tel: 01932 253666
Fax: 01932 252777
(for organic seeds, wooden worm-
eries, Pot Maker, seaweed extract,
Organic Gardening Catalogue,
organic seed-sprouting grains)

Henry Doubleday Research Association (HDRA)

Ryton Organic Gardens
National Centre for Organic
Gardening
Ryton-on-Dunsmore
Coventry CV8 3LG
Tel: 02476 303517
(for wooden wormeries, Heritage
Seed Library)

Simpson's Seeds

27 Meadowbrook
Old Oxted, Surrey RH8 9LT
Tel/fax: 01883 715242

Suffolk Herbs

Monks Farm
Coggeshall Road
Kelvedon, Essex CO5 9PG
Tel: 01376 572456
Fax: 01376 571189
(for organic seeds, Compost-a-
Cube, Bio Pest Pistol, organic seed-
sprouting grains)

Recycle Works

The Rookery
Chatburn
Clitheroe, Lancs BB7 4AW
Tel/fax: 01200 440600
(for Tiger Worm Compost Bin,
worms)

Ken Muir

Honeypot Farm
Rectory Road, Weeley Heath,
Clacton-on-Sea, Essex CO16 9BJ
Tel: 01255 830181
Fax: 01255 831534
(for self-fertile fruit trees, 'Autumn
Bliss' raspberries)

Mrs Caroline Riden
Caer Estyn Farm
Rhyddyn Hill
Caergwrie
Near Wrexham
Wales LL12 9EF
(for *Crocus sativus* corms, send
an sae for factsheet)

Natural Collection
PO Box 2111
Bath
Avon BA1 2ZQ
Tel: 01225 442288
Fax: 01225 469673
(for Log Maker)

Thrive (formerly Horticultural
Therapy)
The Geoffrey Centre
Beech Hill
Reading
Berkshire RG7 2AT
Tel: 0118 988 5688
Fax: 0118 988 5677
(Battersea Park Thrive centre:
Tel: 020 7720 2212)

Wiggly Wrigglers Limited
Lower Blakemere Farm
Herefordshire HR2 9PX
Freephone: 0800 216990
(for polypropylene sacks, Can-O-
Worms wormery, worms, desktop
Worm World)

G.M. & E.A. Innes
Oldtown
Brownhills, Newmachar
Aberdeenshire AB21 7PR
Tel: 01651 862333
(for a large selection of potatoes)

Webster's
33 School Road
Arbroath, Angus DD11 2LU
Tel: 0241 76071
(for a large selection of potatoes)

C. Rassell Ltd (Harper Products'
'Mushroom Kit')
The Lodge Nursery
80 Earls Court Road
London W8 6EQ
Tel: 020 7937 0481

Interplay UK Limited
Crown Lane
Marlow, Bucks SL7 3HL
Tel: 01628 488944
Fax: 01628 476700
(for anteries, desktop Worm World)

Chiltern Seeds
Bortree Stile
Ulverston, Cumbria LA12 7PB
Tel: 01229 581137
(for a large selection of basil seeds)

Planet Organic
42 Westbourne Grove
London W2
Tel: 020 7221 7171
(for hand-turned and electric
juicers)

Highland Wildwoods
Blackstand
Fortrose
Ross-shire IV10 8SW
Tel: 01381 621040
(for oyster mushroom spawn,
outdoor mushrooms)

books

Salads for Small Gardens
by Joy Larkcom, Hamlyn,
London (contains toxicity
information)

The Sprouters' Handbook
by Edward Caimey, Argyll,
Scotland (contains nutritional and
toxicity information)

The Sprouting Book
by Dr Ann Wigmore, Avery, New
Jersey (contains nutritional
information)

The Wheatgrass Book
by Dr Ann Wigmore, Avery, New
Jersey

index